Dice Setting Crapsability

CHARLES C. WESTCOTT

iUniverse, Inc.
New York   Bloomington

iUniverse books may be ordered through booksellers or by contacting:

iUniverse
1663 Liberty Drive
Bloomington, IN 47403
www.iuniverse.com
1-800-Authors (1-800-288-4677)

Because of the dynamic nature of the Internet, any Web addresses or links contained in this book may have changed since publication and may no longer be valid. The views expressed in this work are solely those of the author and do not necessarily reflect the views of the publisher, and the publisher hereby disclaims any responsibility for them.

ISBN: 978-1-4401-9572-3 (sc)
ISBN: 978-1-4401-9573-0 (ebook)

Printed in the United States of America

iUniverse rev. date: 12/30/2009

Other books by author

Craps Shooters Wake Up and Smell the Roses - 2001
Craps and Smelling the Roses - 2002
Wake Up Craps Shooters - 2006

Web Site

www.diceinstitute.com - 2006

Dice Setting Crapsability

Charles C. Westcott

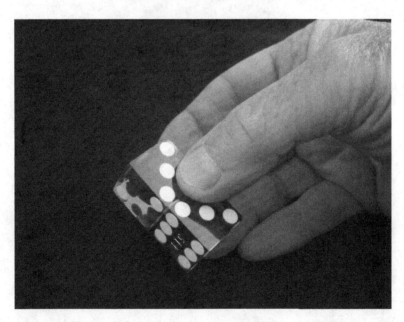

Acknowledgements

This book is dedicated to the dice community and especially to the members of Dice Institute.com, and the Saturday night boat crew. I would especially like to thank Clubsodakenny for proof reading the manuscript and Dice Coach Beau Parker for his kind words in the Forward. Mad Professor, Deadcat, DaveofSA, CSK and Golfer, thanks for the chapter input. Last but not least a special thanks to my son Kevin for providing computer support.

Acknowledgments

Foreword

By Beau Parker- The Dice Coach

As an instructor and coach in the world of dice influence, I am always interested in the thoughts and perspective of others in our field.

I have known Charlie Westcott for several years now, both professionally, and as a friend, and have always enjoyed discussing his views on craps play. It has been my privilege to review this book, and I found it very enlightening. This will be book number four for Charlie and is probably his best yet! +

A must read for all avid players in the game of craps, this book covers all aspects of the game from the beginning of basic play - Betting strategies: right or wrong - money management and bankroll – Discipline - your mental game - casino heat - waiting for and how to recognize a hot hand – to the exotic bets and signature numbers.

Does setting the dice really work? I feel that is does, and with Charlie's input, you can make it work for you too.

I have had the pleasure of playing many enjoyable and profitable sessions with Charlie over the past years; he is one of the dice community's great shooters. Remember this is not a 100 percent science, but does work most of the time. I would not hesitate to bet on Charlie; he is a knowledgeable and disciplined player.

Thank you Charlie for all the hard work and concise input you have given us about the game of craps. Your perspectives have benefited all of us.

Beau Parker, Dice Coach, Las Vegas

About the Author

I have been lucky enough to have read this new book "DICESETTING CRAPSABILITY" by Charles "Charlie009" Westcott who is a dear friend and a fellow Dice Influencer. In this book you will get an inside look at the world of Dice Influencing or Dice Control. Charlie is a veteran advantage craps player, dice influencing instructor, author, and one of the two men who make the "DiceInstitute.com" website run.

In his latest book Charlie describes the game of craps in great detail and how you can also to be a successful Dice Influencer. In the book Charlie provides insight into the actual odds of the game and a look into the world of real casino craps play. The author provides a "how to" guide for Dice Influencing and successful casino play Charlie describes in great detail the requisite knowledge and physical skills necessary to be a successful Dice Influencer.

Charlie writes in an unvarnished style that comes from a man who actually walks the walk in the casinos. Charlie in this book provides a unique window into the world of Dice Influencing. The book begins with Charlie describing the basics of the game for the craps beginner and proceeds to describe the necessary skills, betting strategies, grips, dice sets, and bankroll management of a successful Dice Influencer.

The author in the book also describes in great detail the trip reports from his real life adventures in the casinos with his Saturday

Night at the Boat Crew. The trip reports detailing the "Saturday Night Boat Crew" adventures are written in Charlie's own no-nonsense style. These trip reports are set in the casinos and are written better that any reality show on television. I know these trip reports to be real and described accurately because I was actually present for some of these adventures in the casinos. The author tells it like it is and describes the good times with all the wins as well as the occasional heartbreaking losses at the craps tables.

I hope that you enjoy the book as much as I did!

Club Soda Kenny

Preface

The intention of this book is to encompass the three areas of craps education that will give you the knowledge and tools to become a force at the craps tables. Dice influencing can only be accomplished by dedication to many hours of practice. Understanding all the playing details and how to react to the stumbling blocks and land mines that will be placed in your way will make you a formidable casino foe.

The first area that has to be digested is the understanding of the basics of the game. You must know the different bets available to you and which bets give you the best percentage and opportunity to win. The second area has to do with many phases of play that you should be aware of. You would do well to digest every one of them. Each one in its own way has a message that will help you obtain your goal

The final area has to do with my experiences at the craps tables in the Midwest area and Las Vegas. I have included a vast amount of session reports including adventures on the Midwest boats including the Saturday Night at the Boat series. Player's handles will be used instead of real names for obvious reasons.

I would suggest that you do not skip any chapters or jump around from topic to topic. The first chapter deals with the basics and a review is in order for complete understanding of the game before we get into all the other knowledge you are going to require to become an advantage player. There is a method to my madness so start from the front and don't put the horse behind the carriage.

Hopefully this book will answer any questions you have about becoming proficient as a dice influencer.

Charles C. Westcott

Table of Contents

List of Illustrations

Chapter 1

Part 1 - Basic Craps for Beginners

Craps is the most fascinating casino game out there. Why is it, that most people are intimidated by it and scared to death to try it? Basically it is simple. All you have to do is walk into a casino and look for a crowd of guys standing around an oversize pool table with high sides. Then drop some money on the table and ask for some chips. Then throw a chip on the pass line... wait, stop right there. What's a pass line? How do you ask for chips? Who are these guys in white shirts and bow ties and why does one of them have a stick in his hand?

I guess we better start over! When you approach the crap table, you see the man with the stick with his back to you. He is called the **stickman** or stick person. He controls the flow of the game and uses that hooked stick to rake in the dice after each toss. He directs payoffs from the numbers that are rolled. He also places your "crazy crapper" bets of which we will discuss later. The stickman determines weather your toss of the dice is legal by hitting the far end wall of the table. If you are losing, he might let you get by a couple of times with weak tosses. If you are winning, he sure will be quick to tell you to hit the back wall with the dice.

The lazy guy sitting down across from the stick person is called the **box person** His or her job is to spread out your buy-in money for the camera up above and then stuff it into a little slot in the table in front of him called the drop box. The box person also checks the dice when they fly off the table to make sure they were not switched when returned to the table. He also watches the dealers on each side of him for correct payoffs. When you cash out of the game, he will count your chips and color them up for you, so you don't have to carry so many chips to the cashier's window. The box person also will make sure the **floor manager** gets your player card so they can track your play for comps.

The two persons on each side of the box person are called **dealers**. They are your best friends. Each dealer works half of the craps table. He handles your place bets and come bets. He will make your payoffs on wins and snatch your chips when you lose. The dealer is your main contact with the crap table. Get to know him and befriend him. If you are a beginner crapper and you are, or you wouldn't be reading this chapter, you will find that the dealer can be very helpful. Ask him questions. They are always aware of the weather, wind conditions and hot and cold running tables.

Behind the box person you will see the **floor person.** He's the guy in a suit with a cup of coffee in his hand. He will check your player's card and return it to you personally. This is the crew you well be faced with at the crap table. There also is the **pit boss**, but he is not important to us.

Let's go over this one more time. While you are at the table throwing the dice, the **stick person** watches you. You watch the **dealer** so you get the right payoff. The **dealer** watches you for proper betting. The **box person** watches the **dealer** for correct payoffs. The **floor manager** watches the **box person** so that all that money goes into the drop box. The **pit boss** watches the **floor manager** watch the **box person** watch the **dealers** dance to the tune of the **stick person's banter** and the camera up above records it all. Got that? Let's move on and see what the shooter is all about.

Part 2 - The Shooter Coming Out

The **shooter** is the cat with the dice. The dice move around the table clockwise. The shooter gets to choose two dice from five or six that the stick person pushes in front of you when it's your turn. As soon as you select a pair of dice, you are expected to throw them immediately. Handle them with one hand. That's so the crew will know you are not trying to slip some loaded dice into the game. If you are not ready to shoot, don't pick up the dice. Once you are ready to shoot, set your dice in one hand and throw them toward the other end of the table. Be sure to hit the back wall.

You are now the shooter. You keep throwing the dice until the stickman says in a bored voice, **"Seven and out."** That's it! You're done! Next shooter! If you throw a seven on the come-out roll, you shoot again.

The come-out roll is the shooter's first roll. Once he throws a number other than 7, 11, 12, 2, or 3, a point is established. The shooter then keeps throwing until he makes that number or throws a seven. If he makes the number known as the **point**, he still keeps throwing the dice and is coming out again. He keeps the dice until a seven is rolled after a point is established. How do we know what the point is and if someone is coming out? Well, there is this puck that has white on one side and the word "ON." The other side is black and has "OFF" printed on it. When you arrive at the table, just look for that puck. If it is sitting on a number with the white ON side up, that's the point and we are in the middle of a roll. If the black side is up and sitting in the *don't come* box, the shooter is coming-out.

Part 3 - Craps Table Layout Decoded

Now that we know who is doing what at the table, let's find out what we can do.

Craps tables are like blackjack tables. They have minimum and maximum amounts that you can bet. To find out what the table minimum is, look for the plastic sign on the table wall next to the dealer. Table minimums vary from $2 to $100 depending on your location. On the Vegas strip, they run from $5 to $100 minimum. If you are not sure of the minimum, just ask any of the crew.

The first and most important section on the table layout is the **PASS LINE**. If you do nothing else but put a $5 bet on the PASS LINE, you are now playing craps. You can stand there and wait until there is a decision on that bet. You will either win or lose $5. How do you win? If the shooter (the cat shooting the dice) throws a seven or eleven, you win $5. If he throws a 2, 3, or 12, you lose $5. If he throws any other number, nothing happens but a point is established. If the shooter throws that number again, before a seven is rolled, you win $5. After a point is established, if a seven is rolled, you lose on any come-out roll; the PASS LINE is your best bet. You have 8 chances in 36 of winning! You only have 4 chances in 36 of losing.

The next area you see is the ***Don't Pass***. It is located above the PASS LINE. *Don't Pass* is just the opposite of the PASS LINE. A $5 bet on the *Don't Pass* area will win $5 when a 2 or 3 are thrown. The only way you can lose is if a 7 or 11 appear on the first roll. Keep in mind that the seven will show more than any other number. After the point is established, the only way you can lose is if the shooter makes his point. The odds are in your favor that the seven will show before the shooter makes his point.

Here's another way to look at it. On the come-out roll, you have 3 chances in 36 of winning and 8 chances in 36 of losing when you play the *Don't Come*.

The *Don't Come Bar 12* means just that. You don't win or lose if a twelve is thrown.

Above the *Don't Pass* area you will see the ***Field*** betting area. This is a one-roll bet that one of the Field numbers (2, 3, 4, 9, 10, 11, or 12) will show. You have 16 chances in 36 of winning. You also have 20 ways to lose. This is a bet for he unsuspecting. Not a good bet! The bet looks tempting with the two and twelve paying double, but your chances of hitting is 2 in 36. The other numbers in the **Field** area all pay even money. Next above the Field area is the **COME** betting area. The COME bet can be made after a number is established. After you place your $5 chip in the COME area, the next roll of the dice will determine what will happen to your bet. If a box number (4, 5, 6, 8, 9 or 10) is thrown, your bet is moved to the box with that number in it. It stays there until the number is made and then you win $5 or a seven is thrown in which case you lose $5.

If a seven or eleven appears while your chip is in the COME area you win $5 and your bet can stay in the COME area for the next toss or you can pick it up and cash in.

Two, three or twelve will lose your COME bet, in the COME area. Now pay attention! If your bet now up in one of the COME box numbers wins, the entire amount of your bet plus your winnings will come down and be placed in the COME area closest to you. It's your responsibility to pick up your chips from the COME area and decide if you want to put another COME bet. If you already had a second COME bet put down, then you would be paid just your winnings and the first COME bet would remain in place. This is called off and on. As long as you keep a COME bet on board, the other established COME bets already in their box will stay up. When the seven appears, all the COME bets in the COME box will lose.

You will win your COME bet that is in the COME area. If you think that was easy, wait till we get to the "Odds" bet. Let's jump right into the *Don't Come* bet. That's the little box just to the left of COME box numbers. The *Don't Come* bet is just like the *Don't Pass* bet except it can only be made after a point has been established. It works just the same as the *Don't Pass* bet except you are betting the shooter does not make his point. *Don't Come* bets are placed in the very top of the point box.

Place betting is next on our agenda. The *Place Bet* area is at the bottom and top of the point number area. It's a narrow strip that says *Place Bets*. You so far, have placed all bets in their area. The *dealer must handle the Place Bet.* Simply put your chips on the table and say, "Place the six for $6." The dealer will put your chips in the *six-box* in a precise location to tell him who made the bet. That's right! Your chips are placed in the *six* box directly related to where you are standing at the table.

All *Place Bets* and COME bets are handled this way. Now you know how they know whom to pay off on winners. We will go into Place betting in great depth a little later. Just outside the big box in the center of the table you will see a bunch of circles with C and E's in them. The C stands for Craps (2, 3, and 12) and the E stands for eleven.

To make a **C & E** bet, just toss a couple chips to the stickman and say, "C & E please!" This gives you a one-roll chance at winning.

The "C" will pay you 7 to 1, but you only have one chance in nine to win. The "E" will pay you 15 to 1 but you only have one chance in eighteen to win. Each pair of C & E circles represents a player location at the table. By themselves, these bets are bad news. Beginners should stay away from them.

Part 4 - Proposition Bets

On the corner of the table layout, you will see a **Big 6 and 8**. This bet can be made any time and is a working bet until a seven is thrown. It pays even money and should never be bet. Put simply, it's a dumb bet. If you get caught making the **Big 6** or **Big 8 bet**, you will be rated something less than a beginner. Don't play it.

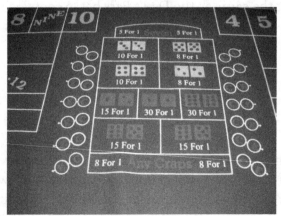

Proposition bets are located in the center of the table layout. First you have the **HARD-WAYS**. Hold it! What's a HARD-WAY? When pairs of two, three four or five show, it is called making the point four the hard way. It pays 7 to 1 and the bet stays working until a seven is thrown or the four is made with a one-three or three one .A pair of fives Pays 7 to 1 and the bet will work until the seven shows or a four-six or six-four pops up. A pair of three's or four's works the same except they pay 9 to 1. The reason for the higher payoff is because you lose when the 2-4, 1-5, 4-2, 5-1, or seven shows. In case of the eight, you lose when 3-5, 2-6, 5-3, 6-2 or seven shows.

Here's some thing to remember if you must make those bets! If you win, the stickman will leave your initial bet up unless you ask for it to be taken down. It is also the stickman's job to point out your winnings to the dealer so he can pay you. I do not recommend playing HARD-WAYS at any time.

That's not to say that I never played a HARDWAY. A few years back, before I began "smelling the roses" at the crap table, I was losing a few chips when my son showed up at the table. He is a notorious HARDWAY player. He doesn't have the patience to play a **"wait and fire"** game. As soon as he got the dice, he told me to jump on the HARD SIX. Just to humor him, I put $5 on the HARD SIX.

As you probably guessed, he threw a HARD SIX. I was amazed when he come right back with another HARD SIX. He said, "Leave it there, I'm hot."

Two throws later he rolls another HARD SIX. Now I was impressed, but I was starting to think about the odds of this continuing. I told the stickman to move my HARD SIX to the HARD EIGHT. A couple of rolls later he popped with the HARD EIGHT. I was $180 ahead on just HARD-WAY bets when he seven-out. This was a rare event and won't happen very often.

Back to some more bad bets that are located in the center of the table. *Any Craps* pays 7 to 1. Bad bet!

Any Seven pays 4 to 1. Bad bet! **Two** or *Twelve* will pay 30 to 1. Bad bet! **Three** or **Eleven** will pay 15 to 1. Bad bet! All these bets are one-time rolls. Don't make them! They are the worst bets on the layout.

You are going to hear someone make a **Horn** bet. It's a one roll bet on the 2, 3, 11, and 12 on the next roll. Four chips must be bet. If you should get lucky and hit on one of those four numbers, you lose the other three bets. Very bad bet!

Part 5 - Free Odds

What in the world is a free **ODDS** bet? It's not even marked on the table layout. The **ODDS** bet is the best bet you can make at craps. It's so good that the casinos want you to be confused as to where and how to play it.

If you have noticed, all the bad bets are clearly marked with the odds. The worst bets are in the center of the table. Wouldn't you think they would mark the area below the PASS LINE as the ODDS betting area? The most frequent question I get by players alongside of me when I am playing is, "Why are you putting chips behind the PASS LINE?" Now try to explain to a beginner in the middle of a crap game about true odds on each number and why you should bet it. I hope this book will clear up all those questions.

The **ODDS** bet is made behind your PASS LINE bet after a point has been established. Remember, the point can only be a 4, 5, 6, 8, 9 or 10. Once a point has been established, you may put an ODDS bet below the PASS LINE, just behind your PASS LINE bet.

How much can you put there? Again we can refer to the plastic sign telling us the table minimum. The bottom of the sign will say Double Odds, 5 X Odds or even 100 X Odds. If it says "Double Odds," you may put twice the amount behind the PASS LINE that you bet on the PASS LINE. How do we benefit from making the ODDS bet? The bet pays true odds on the number trying to be made. If the point was ten and then made, we would win twice the amount we bet behind the line because the true odds are 2 to 1. At the same time we only win even money bet on the PASS LINE.

How do we come up with 2-1 odds on the four and ten? Since there are six ways to roll a seven and only three ways to roll a four or ten, the result is 6 to 3 or 2 to 1 odds. The five and nine would pay 3 to 2 because there are six ways to make seven and four ways to make a five or nine, resulting in 3 to 2 odds.

The six and eight would pay 6 to 5 because there are six ways to make a seven and five ways to make a six or eight resulting in 6 to 5 odds.

We should note that once this odd bet is made, it could be taken down at any time. I don't suggest you take your odds down, once placed. By making the bet, you have reduced the house advantage to about 0.6% at a double odds table. Now that you are totally confused, let's jump to taking **Odds** on the COME bet.

Once you're COME bet goes up to one of the come boxes, you can take your double ODDS on that bet. All you have to do is set two chips on the table and say to the dealer, "ODDS on my ten" or what ever number your COME bet is going to. The dealer will take your two chips and place them on top of your come bet in the box, hanging ¼ over the edge of the original come bet. If you play the PASS LINE or make COME bets, you should always take your ODDS.

Many times I have witnessed a player put three chips or $15 on the pass line and then place three chips or $15 behind the line for his ODDS bet. Don't let me catch you doing that. Think about it! You're at a double odds table! The point is ten and is rolled. You would be paid even money on the pass line, $15. You also would be paid 2 to 1 for the ODDS bet or $30. This would result in a total payoff of $45.

Now, let's back up and only put $10 on the pass line and take $20 ODDS instead. We are betting the same amount of money, $30. Now we win $10 even money on the pass line if the point is made. We also win 2 to 1 or $40 on our ODDS bet. This is a total of $50. Which is the better bet for the same amount of money wagered? This is **Basic Craps 101**. In later chapters, we will cover good money management.

Taking ODDS on the *Don't Pass* and *Don't Come* bet works the same way except you receive fewer payoffs because the odds are reversed on those bets. For example, if you bet $5 on the *Don't Pass* line, you would have to bet $20 ODDS if the point was four or ten. For the total $25 bet you would be paid $15. That's because the odds are 1 to 2. Remember? There are three ways to make a four or ten and six ways to roll seven.

When you lay odds on the Don't Pass, place them along side your bet, or tilted against your bet. If the point is five or nine, a bet of $5 would entitle you to place $15 ODDS for a 2 to 3 payoff of $15 for both bets. If the point were six or eight, a bet of $5 would entitle you to place $12 ODDS for a 5 to 6 payoff of $10 for both bets.

If you are taking ODDS on the *Don't Come*, you must lie your odds bet down in the *Don't Come* area and ask the dealer to place your ODDS bet.

Taking your ODDS on PASS and COME bets is the smart way to play for the "**right better**." A "**right better**" is one who always bets with the dice, and not against them. The "**wrong better**" is one who bets against the dice. In a later chapter we will discuss the plus and minus of wrong betting.

Part 6 - Table Review

Let's review our first visit to a crap table. If you have made it this far in this book, you are ready to make a couple of simple bets.

We approach one of the tables and look for a comfortable spot to jump in. We want to make sure we are at the opposite ends of the table from the guy with the big fat cigar. But first we check the sign next to the dealer to see if we can afford the table **minimum**. We also note that it is a **double odds** table.

Next we get out one of those crispy $100 bills and throw it on the table and ask for chips. If we have a **player card**, we lay that on the table with our money. The dealer will snatch up the $100 bill and throw it to the box person. The box person will carefully lay the $100 bill out in front of him so the camera in the ceiling can witness your buy in. The box person then shoves the $100 bill into the slot in the table, which descends into the drop-box. Now we know why he is called the box person. The box person then hands your player card to the floor manager.

By this time the dealer has put a pile of chips in front of you. Now it's your turn to do something. You pick up your chips and place them in the grooved rack in front of you. If someone is in the middle of a roll; you can just stand around and watch the action until the shooter sevens-out. If a shooter is about to come-out, you can make your first bet. Just put a red chip on the PASS LINE. You are now shooting craps.

When the shooter establishes a point, you put two red chips behind the PASS LINE, directly behind your PASS LINE bet. That's called taking your ODDS. At this point the floor manager will hand you back your player card and wish you good luck.

What he really means is, "Hurry up and lose the $100 so we can get at those other $100 bills in your wallet."

Should you show up at the table during a good roll, don't hesitate to join in. Just *Place* the six and eight for $6 each. There's a good chance you could win a couple bets while waiting for the shooter to make his point or seven-out.

At this point in your crap career, I don't recommend any other bets until you have digested this entire book. Stay away from the **Center Field** bets and the **Big 6 and 8** on the corner of the layout. Playing the **HARDWAYS** will get you to the **highway** in a hurry. When the dice come around to you and it's your turn to roll, you are in charge. Set the dice the way you want and then throw. Make sure you hit the back end of the table. You control the pace of the game. Don't be intimidated by the stickman trying to rush you. Usually they leave you alone until you get hot with the dice. Then the stickman will try to hurry you to throw so the other players don't have time to press up their bets.

What's pressing your bet mean? Say you have a $6 *Place Bet* on board and you want to increase it! Just say to the dealer, "**Press my six one unit**." Now you have $12 on the six.

Part 7 - Pass and Come Odds Review

Most new crapshooters have a hard time remembering all the various odds and their payoffs on all the numbers. We will go over this several times, until it sinks in. Hopefully you will have a workable knowledge of all the odds.

First let's look at the **PASS LINE** betting. When a seven is rolled on the come-out roll, your bet on the **PASS LINE** will pay even money. You have 6 chances out of 36 of seeing the seven on the come-out roll. You also will win even money, if an eleven is rolled. The eleven has 2 chances in 36 of being rolled.

If a box number (4, 5, 6, 8, 9 or 10) becomes the point and you make your odds bet behind the **PASS LINE**, you will receive true odds payoff if the point is made. If the made point were six or eight, you would be paid 6 to 5. For the ones that are short on math, that's $6 for every $5 you bet behind the **PASS LINE**. There are five ways to make a six and five ways to make eight out of 36 chances.

Remember now, if you are at a double odds table, you can only take your odds two times that of your PASS LINE bet. If the made point were five or nine, you would be paid 3 to 2. That would be $15 for every $10 bet behind the **PASS LINE**. There are four ways to make a five and four ways to make 9 out of 36 chances.

If the made point was four or ten, you would be paid 2 to 1 or $20 for every $10 bet behind the **PASS LINE**. There are three ways to make a four and three ways to make a ten out of 36 chances.

The *Don't Pass* betters will face the same odds in reverse.

Taking **ODDS** on the four or ten would cost you four chips for every one chip you bet on the *Don't Pass* line. To make this bet, you would put your four-chips on the *Pass* bet. For the five and nine you would put three chips for every two bet on the *Don't Pass* line. For the six and eight, Don't Pass betters would take $6 ODDS for every $5 bet. Which means you win only win $5 for every $6 bet. In later chapters we will discuss the pros and cons of *Don't* betting.

COME bet odds pay the same as the PASS LINE odds. You are entitled to take your odds on your come bet when it moves up to the COME number box. To make the odds bet on the COME bet, just tell the dealer you want ODDS on your COME after you place two chips in the COME area. The alert dealer will grab up your bet and place it covering half of your COME bet chip in the COME box for that number. You will notice that the COME bets go to the box with that number in it.

Don't Come bets work the same as the *Don't Pass* bets. They are placed in the top box above your COME box numbers. This all seems pretty intense, but don't give up. The dealers will do most of your thinking for you. After a couple of bets, the dealers in Vegas are pretty good and will note your style of play and remind you of taking ODDS etc.

Part 8 - Reviewing Place Bet Odds

Now we go into a whole new set of odds for *Place Bets*. After the point has been established, you can make a *Place Bet* at any time. Placing the six or eight will cost you an extra dollar for every $5 you bet. Why? So you can receive the correct odds payoff when your six or eight hits. The six and eight pays 7 to 6 for every $6 bet. This is a very good bet for beginners and I highly recommend it. In fact it's so good; it's an intricate part of the strategy we will discuss later. Repeat after me! "**There are ten ways to make a six and eight out of 36 chances**." The two numbers played together, give you the best chance of winning, after a point is established. That's a fact Jack and we will pound on it later. *Placing* the five or nine will get 7 to 5 ($7 for every $5 you bet) and the four or ten will pay 9 to 5. If you are infatuated with a 2 to 1 payoff on the four or ten, you can buy either one for a 5% tax to the casino. Don't do it!

Receiving fewer odds on *Place Bets* is the penalty you pay for being able to pick what number you want and not having to go through the COME.

Part 9 - Reviewing the One Roll Bets

Field bets pay even money except for the two 0and twelve, which usually pay double. The **Big 6 and 8** will pay even money. These are one roll bets and should be avoided at all cost. If you are thinking about betting the six or eight, *Place* it. It will pay you more.

Another one roll bet is the **C & E** bet. The C means any craps (2, 3, or 12) and pays 7 to 1. The **E** stands for eleven and pays 15 to 1. They are usually played together on the come out roll. Don't do it.

Any Seven pays 4 to 1. *Any Craps* pays 7 to 1. **Two** and **twelve** pays 30 to 1. **Three** and **eleven** pays 15 to 1. The **Horn Bet**, 2, 3,

All these one roll bets are bad news. Don't bet them.

Part 10 – Hard-way Review

The final bet is the **Hard-ways**. Crazy Crappers love them. They have that need to shout out, "**Hard Six**," or "**All the Hard-ways**." I guess it helps their ego.

Let's review them! Once again the **Hard-way** can only be made one way, **2-2**, **3-3**, **4-4**, or **5-5**. If you bet the **Hard 6** and 5-1, 1-5, 2-4, 4-2 or seven comes up, you lose. You only have one chance in 36 of winning. The **Hard 4** or **Hard 10** pays 7 to 1. The **Hard 6** or **Hard 8** pays 9 to1. The only good thing about the **Hard-way** is they stay working as long as the Hard-way number doesn't come up. Once the number comes up and it isn't hard, you lose. If the seven shows, you also lose your **Hard-way**. You can bet as little as $1.

A lot of players will tip the dealers by making **Hard-way** bets for them. The dealers would much prefer you made a PASS LINE bet for them. At least they would have 8 chances in 36 of winning.

Part 11 - Table Exit

As they say in poker, "Know when to hold them and know when to fold them!" If you have a bad time at a choppy table, don't hesitate to take your action elsewhere. How do you know it's bad? If everybody has only a few chips in their rack and your chips are dwindling, it's time to leave.

If you have lost 75% of your buy-in, be ready to exit left. Don't chase your losses! Remember this! Scared money loses and smart money wins. Above all, **don't gamble with money you cannot afford to lose**.

Now, if someone has just finished a hot roll and your chips are piled up, it's also time to think about making a discreet exit. Unless you have spotted a good roller coming up, I would suggest you **color-up** your chips and cash in.

Now, what does **color-up** mean? When you are ready to leave a table with all your winnings, just ask the dealer to color you up. Place your chips in neat stacks on the table so the dealer can slide them over to the lazy guy sitting down, called the box person. The box person will count your chips and tell the dealer to give you larger denomination chips to carry to the cashier's cage.

It's always smart to count your chips before handing them over to the dealer. The box person will look at you and give you a total. It should jive with your count. If you have a sizable win, toss the dealer a chip and head for the cashier's cage. Where in the devil is the cashier's cage? You will usually find it in some remote spot in back of the casino. This is so maybe you will lose some of those chips before finding the cashier area.

Now that we have cashed in our chips, let's see if we can find the front door! We will have to go through a maze of slot machines, poker machines, blackjack tables and other games waiting to sidetrack our exit. We might even stumble into the sport's book or keno area. This is all by design to keep you gambling. Try finding window or clock in a casino. I have enough trouble just finding the restrooms. Once you learn Craps 101, you will be ready to take the next step towards Dice Influencing.

Chapter 2

Part 1 – Do You Have the Tools?

This is a part by part collection of tools you will need to become an accomplished dice influencer.

The first thing to consider is your knowledge of the basic's of craps. Do you understand all the bets on the lay-out? Do you know what the odds are on all the bets? Do you know what a "fire bet" is or what about "four rolls, no seven"? How about "hopping sevens?"

Going further, you must have control over your **money management**. Do you have a sufficient bank-roll that is not earmarked for other necessities of life? If your answer is yes to these questions, then you can move forward to the next step.

First let's understand that there is no absolute control over the dice. What we are looking for is a **consistent toss** that will allow us enough control to change the expectation odds to our favor. To accomplish this and move to the next level, will require many hours of practice.

You must learn about those two cubes you have in your hand. Opposite sides of the dice always add up to **seven**. You need to know what the opposite number is for every side of the dice. This will help you set the dice faster on the numbers you want. Setting

17

the dice should become second nature to you. Once you have **the dice set**, you must know how to pick them up to satisfy your grip. There are half dozen good grips to be experimented with to determine which is best for you.

The most important thing to be learned is **the toss**. It takes hours and hours of practice to get it down pat. You must develop a starting point and a release point and land the dice in a specific landing area. Speed, height, rotation and distance all play a part in the good controlled toss.

Your **position at the table** is also a factor and should be determined by practice. Right and left of the stick person are usually the preferred positions to shoot from, because of the shorter distance to the back wall. The size of the table also is a factor. Shooting SR-1 or SL-1 on a fourteen foot table is the same as shooting from SR-2 or SL-2 on a twelve foot table.

You will need a **practice rig**. You can buy them or make one. Converted pool tables will also work. If you're loaded with dough, you can buy a real casino style crap table with all the trimmings.

Record keeping of your progress is a must. Putting "Bone Tracker" to work in your arsenal will help justify your means.

All this fore mention detail is to give you an idea of what a dedicated dice setter must go through to become an **advantage player**. The main object of all this, is to be able to throw one, two, three less sevens than the "random expectation roller" throws. Just throwing one less seven in the expected six for thirty-six, will turn the casino odds in your favor.

Above all you have to have **patience,** fortitude to practice and the willingness to accept setbacks along the way. You want to be a low key player and not draw attention to yourself.

All of the points in this chapter can be gone over in great depth on the Dice Institute website. If you skip any of the items discussed, you will fail. You can take it one step further and join the Dice Institute "Message Board/Forum" where answers to all your questions can be had from dice influencing players who have been there.

Part 2 – Taking That First Step

What are the first steps to take as an inspiring dice setter? Take it one step at a time.

First find the **grip** that is comfortable. Then practice picking up the dice so they line up parallel to the back wall. Develop a slow smooth toss and practice this every day until it becomes second nature to you.

You should land the dice six to eight inches from the wall. The next step is to start **setting the dice.** Instead of counting sheep at night, count the sides of the dice so you know the cube front and backwards. 1 & 6 = 7, 2 & 5 = 7 etc. Don't worry about speed for now. The next step is **set, grip and toss** on a routine basis.

Find or make up a **tally sheet**. You can use the hard way set or the V3 to start out. Use the same set for the entire series of tosses. I suggest you toss 36 times or more per practice. I started out tossing 144 a day. You are now ready to record your tosses and figure out your SRR. A random roller is expected to toss 6 sevens in 36 rolls. Your first goal should be 5 sevens or less in 36 rolls. When you have at least 1,000 tosses recorded and have a SRR of 7.0 or more you are ready to test the water.

We can talk about money management and betting later. One step at a time!

Chapter 3

Table Position

How many times have you walked into a casino and found only one spot open at the craps table? You rush over to the spot and immediately bought in and placed a bet? Sound familiar? Been there, done that! That is a big mistake! If there is more than one table, take time to make a careful selection of where you play. Table selection is just as important as table position.

Look for table energy. Seek out a table that is upbeat. Are the players having a good time? Do they have a lot of chips in front of them? Is the table crew friendly and efficient? Are there a lot of high fives and cheering going on? That's the table to hang around and try to play at. Never be in a hurry to lose your money. Don't force yourself into a losing game, just because there was a spot open at the table. Look for the happy go lucky table with energy.

Stay away from the table where most of the players are short on chips and the **Don't** players are loaded. Keep your eye open for another DI. You can always use a little support.

Once you have found the table you would feel comfortable at, its time to maneuver into your best table position. The best table positions are the one's that are the closest to the back wall of the table. Right and left of the stick person is the best. You want to be in position to make the shortest roll possible. Take your time to wait until you can get your favorite spot.

Here is something to remember. If the noise has been going on for awhile at a certain table, be careful. The big run could be just about over and you missed most of it.

Again the best possible positions to play from are stick right (SR1 and 2) and stick left (SL1 and 2). It's your decision on where you feel most comfortable.

In my experience, I have had wonderful luck, playing on Saturday nights and getting my SR1 position. When I arrive at one of my favorite Boats, I check all the tables for energy. Usually I zero in on one particular table and hang around watching the action. On several occasions one of the table crew would ask other shooters to move over so I could shoot from SR1.

Only once did a young dude hesitate to move. The stick guy told him that if he wanted to have a good chance to make some money tonight, let him shoot from that spot. Boy, did he put me on the spot. The dude moved and I was apprehensive about my turn with the dice. The dice gods must have been watching and allowed me four points. The dude that moved said I could shoot in his place any time.

Chapter 4

Are You Ready?

Are you ready for the next step in dice setting? If you have prepared yourself properly, you will go to the table with confidence, ready to journey into the world of craps.

If **you are ready** for the next step, then let's move forward. If you have done all the things suggested in Chapter 2 and feel like you want to try your new found skill in the real world in a casino, then give it a try. There will be a big difference playing in a casino than practicing at home. You will be faced with new situations and distractions. Finding a table to your liking won't be easy. **Finding a table** with your position open is sometimes very difficult. Now days with more and more dice setters out there, the preferred positions are often occupied. You must be patient and wait for a position you will feel comfortable shooting from.

Once you take up your **position at the table**, don't be in a hurry to buy in. Make sure you know the table minimum. Make note of the amount of chips in everybody's rack. There might be a reason for your position opening up. The guy next to you might be an obnoxious, cigar smoking jerk that has been upsetting the table. Your position may have come open because the shooter seven-out and left.

Table Positions

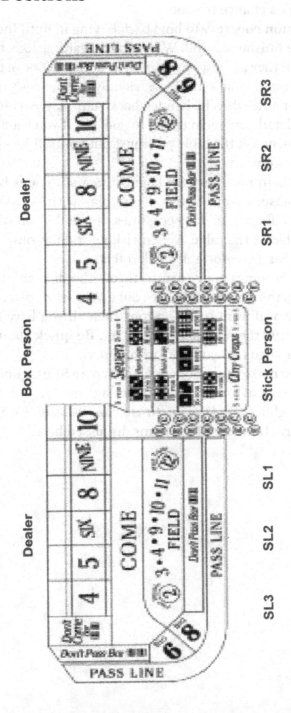

Now you will have to wait for the dice to go all around the table before you get a chance to shoot.

It's **common courtesy** to hold back buying in until the person with the dice finishes his roll. While you're waiting, look the crew over and see if they are responsive to their duties. Is one of the Suits hanging around the table and is he friendly. Did he wish you good luck by your name when he handed back your players card?

All this detail may seem trivial to you, but if you want to have a good experience at the table you must put yourself in a position to participate comfortably.

Another item necessary for comfort is a **sufficient bankroll** so you can absorb some losses. Don't play with scared money that is needed for day to day necessities. If you do, you will never be comfortable at the table. When risking money, only you can determine what a comfortable bank roll is.

When it becomes your turn to throw the dice and the stick person passes the dice to you to pick out a pair, select two that have numbers that you want to set on top. Then all you have to do to set them is twist them around to your set. **Be quick about it**, but methodical and go into your pickup and toss.

When you make your come-out bet, make a $1 pass line **bet for the crew**. Treat it as an insurance policy against future heat.

All throughout the *Dice Institute.com* website you will find detailed instructions on all the items discussed here.

Chapter 5

Part 1 – Scared Money

Playing with scared money? When scared money plays! What is scared money? Scared money can come in several ways. It can be the money you bring with you to the table.

It may not be enough for the level of play you are anticipating at the table minimum you are playing at. The money you brought to the table may have been ear marked for food, rent or a car payment. Under these conditions you are going to be worried about losing and your frame of mind will be negative.

Negative thoughts will prevent you from making the right bets at the right time and cause you to make wrong bets chasing your lost money. You need a bankroll of money that is not needed for any other purposes and can be lost without putting a financial burden on your family.

The size of your bankroll depends on your **comfort zone** and what you feel you need to survive some loses and keep yourself in a position to recover your losses. Each individual will be different. Some of you will be able to play with a small bankroll and will have modest wins and losses. Myself, I feel I need three to four times what I am willing to lose to maintain my comfort zone.

How do we recognize other people's scared money? They are very easy to identify. When someone comes up to the table with four or five chips in his hand and doesn't put them on the rack, he is holding scared money or what's left of his scared money. Don't bet on him.

Another one is the guy that pushes his way into the table and throws $20-$30 of crumpled up bills on the table and bets it all on the field. Another scared money loser!

Then there is the guy who doesn't make a bet till he gets the dice. He puts his two chips on the PL and then shakes rattle and fling the dice as hard as he can to the other end of the table. He stood by and watched three DI's in front of him have decent hands. He should have taken notes.

How about the loud mouth at the end of the table that keeps yelling for hard-ways and has no other bets? He's shooting for the moon. If he wasn't playing with scared money, he would be making more intelligence bets.

If you are scared to make the bet, don't make it. **Sufficient bankroll** is just as important as your grip, set and toss

Part 2 – Bankroll

The amount of your bankroll will be directly related to your comfort zone and affordability bankroll size. Once the scared money issue is out of the way we can concentrate on what is an intelligent amount of money to be put at risk.

The size of the bankroll per session will be directly related to the table minimum and your affordability. Your ability as an advantage player will also be taken into account along with the average number of players at the table. My style of betting and managing money may not coincide with your style and should be seen as an example only.

When playing at the boats we usually end up playing at crowded tables and at the mercy of what's available to us. The minimum rated tables are usually $5, $10, $15 and $25. A $10 table being the most common! The tables usually average ten shooters. For the following examples we will say that I am the only DI at the table.

When at a rare $5 table, I would buy in for $200-$300 and that buy-in would be my stop loss figure for that session. By betting a $5 pass-line or $6 place six on each player at the table would be the worst case scenario. I would be able to play two complete rounds without winning. The other $100 would be used for my betting only when I had the dice. This will keep me at the table in play for close to two hours.

One or two of the random rollers might make you a few bucks and if you do your thing, you should survive for awhile till lightning strikes. How you handle the wins is a matter of money management. Making the most out of our bankroll is our main concern.

If at a $10 table, I would buy in for $400 with a stop-loss set at $300. I would use $200 for betting on the random rollers and $100 on myself. No more than $50 per turn with the dice.

If at a $15 table, I would buy in for $500 with a stop-loss set at $400. I would have $300 available for betting on the random rollers and $100 on myself.

At a $25 table buy in for $1,000 and set my stop loss at $600. For This level of play check with the Mad Professor and have your heart checked.

When in Las Vegas my buy-in is usually double the figures mentioned above. This is for comp purposes at the hotel I'm staying at. My stop-loss figures are pretty much the same.

Learn to play within you're bank roll and heed your stop-loss figure. You will be surprised at how far your bankroll will go.

Remember, it's not the size of the bankroll that counts, it's the way you apply the bankroll. Make sure you have a bankroll survival plan in place.

Eliminate scared money. Build a bankroll from surplus funds and then insert your money management plan.

Chapter 6

Dice Sets

The setting of the dice should become second nature to the aspiring dice influencer. To understand and practice this, we must know that all opposite sides of the dice add up to seven. This knowledge is especially useful prior to the setting of the dice. When we see a six on top of a die, we know a one is on the bottom. If we see a two on top, we know a five is on the bottom, etc. It's just a matter of adding to what we see, to total seven. This tells us what is on the opposite side of that die.

With a little practice, you should be able to set the dice within five seconds, give or take a second. Don't worry, you won't be the slowest. Everybody else around you will be fumbling around with the dice a lot longer than you. You can speed up your setting time if you watch the dice being delivered to you by the stick person. By the time you receive the dice, you will know the adjustments you have to make to get the set you want to use.

There are six basic sets and various permutations of these sets that are available for you to use. These basic sets are composed of either two or four potential sevens in their make up. The sets with only two potential sevens are the one's that you should give most of your attention to. Sets that have four potential sevens can be used on the come-out. These seven laden sets are also useful to C&E and Horn betters on the come-out. Here are the six basic sets and two of the most used permutations:

The Six Basic Sets

Part 1 – All 7's Set

The **ALL 7's set** is your best come-out set. It has sevens on all sides and even on the ends of the dice which means it has a high potential of you throwing a seven. The ALL 7's set is the most powerful when in a DI's hand because he has a better chance of throwing the big red than the random roller. If you're off axis, you usually have a chance to end up with a six or eight for your point. Another point to be noted is that your expectation of throwing 2, 3 or 12 is very low. You don't want to be on the C&E or Horn bet when a DI is setting the ALL 7's set. You will see very few elevens. Always try and see what other DI's are setting and if it is the seven set, bet accordingly.

Part 2 V-3

The **V-3 set**, also known as the **Flying V-3 set**, is probably the most popular with the dice community. It only has two potential sevens and places the two most powerful numbers, six and eight on the sides. If you are a six and eight place better, this quarter turn of the six to the top, you will have all the inside numbers on the sides of the dice.

There are several adjustments you can make to the V-3 to satisfy you're needs and blend in with you're toss. As long as you don't change the axis (2/5, 1/6) you still will be throwing a permutation of the V-3. You can roll both dice over to satisfy your end results, as long as you keep the same axis.

Part 3 V-2

The **V-2 set** is some times called the **MINI V-2 set**. It is similar to the V-3. It has only two potential sevens in it's make up, which makes it a very usable set. This set is good for going after fours and tens. It has two fours and two tens on the sides. By rotating the left die, with the three facing you, one quarter of a turn you will have the inside numbers on all four sides. Again you must keep the same axis (6/1, ¾) through out any change you try.

If you are having trouble sniping out fours or tens with the mini V on top, rotate both die a quarter or half turn forward and see if your results improve. When you find a set that's working, stick with it until it goes bad and then make a change.

Part 4 – X-6's

X-6's or CROSS SIXES set is the third point cycle set that has an expectation distribution of two sevens. It rides on a 2-5, 4-3 axis with a vertical six on the top, left and a horizontal six, on the top right. You have the 4-5 facing you. The set can be turned around or rolled over for the best results. This set is good for all inside numbers but has a high instance of junk numbers. This makes for long hands with not much profit. A good time to use this set is when you have the Iron Cross in play. This would bring the **Field Bet** into play and all those trash numbers can be capitalize on.

Part 5 – S-6's

S-6 or STRAIGHT 6 set has an expectation distribution of four sevens. It is great for the come-out toss. It rides the 3-4/3-4 axis and has a high incident of C&E and Horn numbers. The six's when placed end to end, look like a railroad track. You can have the two's or fives facing you. The important thing is to keep the same axis. The set has two hard-ways on the sides along with the six's and aces. The potential distribution factor for this set is interesting. The expectation of the 2 and 12 showing is 1 time each. For the 3 and 11, 2 each. For the 4 and 10, 1 each. For the 5 and 9, 0 each. For the 6 and 8, 2 each. For the 7, 4 times! This set can be very beneficial on your come-out play. You have a high expectant seven and, low numbers.

Part 6 - P-6's

P-6's or PARALLEL 6's has an expectation distribution of four sevens. It rides on a 5-2, 5-2 axis and is used by "Don't" players on the come-out. The sixes line up parallel to each other on top. You will have threes or fours facing you. Don't expect to throw any elevens with this set due to the expectation distribution of zero. This may be one of the six primary sets but I don't see any good use.

Part 7 – The Hard-way

HARD-WAY set is a permutation of the ALL 7's set. You will see that when you have 4/3 on top and 5/2 towards you, all you have to do is turn one die a half turn and you have the HARD-WAY set. Think about that for a minute. If you are throwing the HARD-WAY set and double pitch, you end up with a seven. When throwing the HARD-WAY set you have the potential of four sevens. It's a good set to practice with, to see how often you throw primary numbers (Hard-ways). Keep track of how many times you throw HARD-WAYS in 36 tosses. You might think twice before throwing or betting on it in a casino.

Part 8 – Inside Numbers

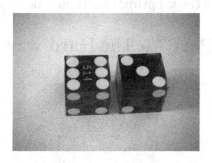

INSIDE NUMBERS set is a permutation of the V-3. It rides on a 2-5, 1-6 axis (just like the V-3). The fastest way to set it up is to set for the V-3 and then rotate the six facing you one quarter turn so you have 6-3 on top. You now have the inside numbers on all sides of the dice. This move confuses the hell out of the stick and box personnel. This set results in very few junk numbers. It's best used for just the point cycle.

Chapter 7

Logical Sets

Setting logically when making smart bets will set you apart from the random shooters. Too often, when your shooting has gone bad or you are in a slump, you succumb to the advice of others. That advice could be to change your set, grip, toss, speed and even shooting position. For now let's just analyze the set. A lot of shooters use the same set for the come-out and the point. The most common being the hard-way set. The way the hard-way set is made up, you have a pair of two's, three's, four's and fives on the four sides of the dice. The set is derived from the all sevens set. Both sets have an expectancy of four sevens. Not good except for using the all sevens set for the come-out. With the hard-way set you only have one way to make a four, six, eight or ten hard-way number while those four expected sevens are a threat. Setting for a hard-way doesn't appeal to me at one chance in thirty-six of making hard-way number. Now if your point is a hard-way number, why would you want to use a set allowing you only one primary possibility? Let's not forget that our goal is to keep the dice on axis.

Logical Smart Set

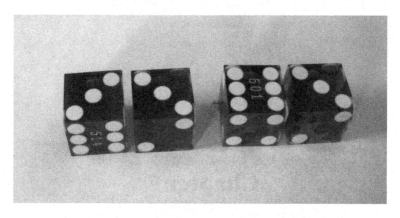

When we are keeping the dice on axis, we want to have two opportunities to make our point no matter what the point is. Using the V-3 gives you two primary chances of making a six or eight when your toss is on axis. The V-2 will give you two primary chances of making the four or ten when your throw is on axis. If you are hitting your primary numbers and your point is five or nine, you might try setting for them to hit when you are throwing a good on axis toss. If you are in a betting position with all the inside numbers covered, you might try setting the V-3 and rotating the six ¼ turn forward so that the six is on top. With an on axis toss you will have a chance to throw a five, six, eight or nine with one of the four inside numbers on each side of the dice. The beauty of these sets is they have only two expected sevens. Use the set that will give you the best results and when it is working, don't change a thing. The odds are stack against us and we need all the help we can get. Set logically and bet smart.

Chapter 8

Setting to Enhance Your Play

It's time to learn how to change your dice sets to give you a chance to avoid the seven and enhance your shooting for optimal results.

How you set the dice is the first step before the grip and making the all important toss. You want to use sets that minimize the chances of coming up seven. A lot of shooters will use the same set for everything and not realize the potential of varying the set for optimal play for certain box numbers.

You should use a least two basic sets. I use five. I suggest you use the all sevens set for your come-out roll. That's the set that has sevens on all four sides and on the ends. Once you have a point, you can go to your favorite set or "chase the point." If you are using your favorite set and it is producing for you, stay with it. Like they say, **"if it aren't broke don't fix it."**

I like to **"chase the point."** If the point is four or ten, I will set the V-2. Two sides of the dice will have a four and two sides will have a ten. For the point of six and eight, I will use the V-3. Two sides have a six and two have an eight.

For the five and nine, I will use my permutation of the V-3, where I have a five, six, eight or nine on each side of the dice. This set is especially good for hitting inside numbers. Another little

37

trick I use involves **"losing the seven."** There are nights when I can't make a six for the life of me. Even a random roller is expected to make a six every 7.2 tosses. I know if I keep throwing that V-3, the seven is going to catch up with me. So to confuse the seven, I rotate the dice from what I have been setting so I don't have the same number on top all the time. If the stick person presents the dice to me with the fours on top, I will just turn the dice so the six, two or one, five is facing me and grip and rip.

One popular set I will never use is the Hard-way set. The four potential sevens the set has is enough to scare me off. The set, in my opinion, is only good for practice to see if you are hitting primary numbers with your on axis toss.

One more set I would bring to your attention is the S-6 (straight 6's). It's the come-out set I use when making a C&E bet. I put the six, five on top and the two, one towards me. If you can keep it on axis, you well get some elevens or threes. I seldom use the cross-six's. Too many junk numbers come up for my taste.

The parallel 6's is too rich in sevens. Not for me!

Find the best sets you feel comfortable with and can set easily. If results are not forthcoming, don't be scared to change sets. **If it's broke, fix it.**

Chapter 9

The Grip

The grip is the second element that sets you up for a good toss. It's all a matter of choice, comfort and execution. Choose what is best for you physically and not what someone else is using or recommending. Copying someone else's grip because he is getting better results won't help you if you are not physically able to handle his grip. With a grip suited to you and with the proper mechanics, your efforts will be rewarded.

Once you have settled on a grip that is comfortable, then it's just a matter of moving your fingers up or down on the dice to adjust amount of spin you require too stay on axis.

The Pickup

3 Finger Grip

The 3 Finger grip is very popular with the Advantage Player because of its ease to put into play.

2 Finger Grip

2 Finger assist

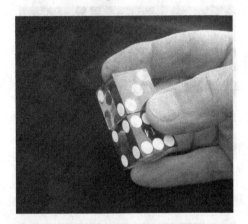

1 Finger Grip

Full 3 Finger Grip

4 Finger Grip

4 Finger Top View

Pincer Grip

Ice Tong Grip

Chapter 10

Part 1 - The Toss

The toss or delivery of the dice is the most important element in dice setting influencing.

The first element is the setting of the dice which can be any set and does not affect the toss (see Chapter 5). The second element is the grip which can be one of several that feel right to you (see Chapter 8). The third element is the toss, which I feel is the most important part of influencing good results.

The consistency of your delivery is your main concern. Any set or grip may be used but only a consistent throw will give you repeating results.

The casinos have five rules for throwing the dice. How each casino interprets these rules, will very as you will see.

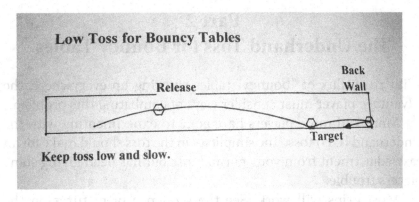

The **Underhand Toss** using the Three Finger Grip and the V-3 Set.

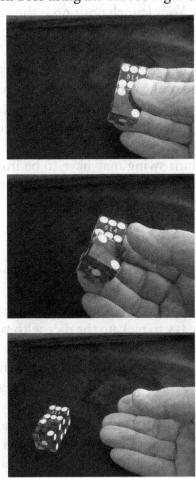

Part 2
The Underhand Toss for Bouncy Tables

With the influx of "bouncy" tables showing up everywhere, the advantage player must consider ways of combating this problem.

More and more players have gone to experimenting with the Underhand (UH) toss. The simplicity in the toss should make for an easy adjustment from your normal toss but has been giving some players trouble.

Most grips will work. See the sequence of pictures on the previous page. It's just a matter of turning your hand so the palm is up instead of down. Your launch position is the same and can start from the table top or a few inches above the table. It's important that your chest be facing the back wall.

At release the dice should roll off your fingers with a little forward spin instead of the usual backspin. The forward motion of your hand will impart part a little forward spin or maybe no spin at all. The secret is to toss it low and slow so the dice has just enough energy to get to the back wall.

A small pendulum swing may have to be inserted in the toss to get you to the back wall. Don't push or flick the dice forward. Remember low and slow to go.

Part 3
Casino Craps Toss Rules

Rule Number 1: *Use only one hand to set and pick up dice.* Did you ever see anyone try to pick up the dice with two hands? I don't think so. Once I did see a woman pick up all five dice and throw them down the table. I guess she thought we were playing yahtze. Once you have picked the dice up, try switching hands with the dice. The pit critters in $300 suits will be all over you, thinking you are switching to loaded dice. I get a kick out of the guy who shakes the dice up by his ear before he throws. What is he listening for? Probably his inner voice was on a metaphysical plane giving off an organic vibration of energy from another dimension. Just use one hand for every thing.

Rule Number 2: ***Toss in air above table.*** Sounds simple enough! There's plenty of air above the table. Some casinos might tell you to keep your toss below the stick persons head. Others might get on you for trying to slide the dice on the layout to the back wall. They even put in speed bump wires under the felt. They are more tolerant on low tosses as long as you get one bounce before the wall. What do they consider above the table? Is it the chip rail or the layout? The box guy will tell you in a hurry if you are doing it wrong in his eyes.

Rule Number 3: ***Must bounce at least once on table.*** This is not a problem for the dice influencer. He is throwing a controlled shot at a specific area with each toss. Your random rollers are all over the place with their tosses and some are off the table more than on. The DI knows that the bounce is what counts.

Rule Number 4: ***Both dice must hit back wall.*** This is my favorite. I love it when one of the dice come up short of the wall and one of the suits goes nuts and yells at the shooter about hitting the wall with both die. For the life of me I can't understand why these over zealous pit critters get so upset about both dice hitting back wall. They don't realize that the dice setter's main goal is to hit the back wall equally with both die. They should take a course in dice setting and then they would know when one die falls short of the back wall, the roll becomes random. Isn't that what the casinos want? The short comings of the floor managers are only superseded by their underlings playing big shot and not knowing the game.

Rule Number 5: ***No additive's allowed on the dice.*** You can leave your three and one oil at home and don't spit on the dice. My favorite is under arm deodorant. I got that one from a GTC trained player who put a chunk in a rough compact. Just before his turn to shoot, he would put his hand into his pocket and get some deodorant on his finger tips. He would rub his grip fingers real good so you would never notice it. The finger tips were perfectly dry for his turn with the dice.

That's it! Five simple rules interpreted twenty-five different ways by the casinos.

Part 4 - The Toss Flight

There are two lines of thought on how high you should throw the dice.

Most DI's will start off on a thirty to forty-five degree accent, when they release the dice. With all the bouncy tables around, I find the lower arc more productive.

My feeling is the higher you throw the dice, the more chance there is for error. When the dice come from a high toss, they have a tendency to bounce high or scatter. The low arc gives me more control going into the back wall. It's a lot easier to hit your target area.

The high arc is a beautiful thing to watch when it works. When it's not working, things can get ugly. It is easier to keep the dice on axis over a shorter distance than trying to keep control over the high arc.

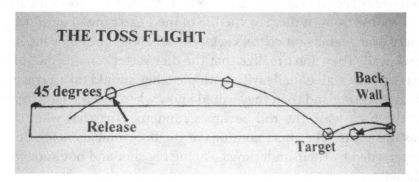

48

Part 5 - The Release Point

Now you need a landing zone. You must pick out a target to throw at. I like to throw at the back pass line, about one foot left of center. Hitting your target area every time will enhance your chance of repeating numbers. The object here is consistency. We want to repeat the same set, same grip, same toss, same speed and spin. Hit the same target area and get the same kick back from the back wall. Sound hard to do? It sure is and it won't come easy without a lot of practice.

The next thing we have to worry about is keeping the dice on a rotating axis through out the toss flight. Keeping the dice on axis is extremely important to the DI. We keep the dice together and rotating equally all the way to the landing zone. With the right speed and a soft landing we enhance the chance of a good result.

Part 6 - Breathing

I never thought of breathing as being a part of the game of craps. For most people breathing comes naturally and they never give it a second thought. I'm one of those guys that never give it a second thought. I have enough to think about when tossing the dice.

There is a whole school of thought out there about taking that deep breathe and exhaling it just before you toss the dice. This is a good thing if you come to the craps table all tensed up and not relaxed. That deep breathe can relax you and help release the tension you might be feeling.

I come to the table relaxed, no tension and only have one thing on my mind. That's to get my hands on the dice and accumulate the casino's chips. I ignore the table crew's banter and the foolishness of the other players at the table.

If you are all tensed up when you receive the dice, take that big breathe and let some of that tension escape before the toss. You see baseball players do it all the time. Basketball players do it before shooting that free throw.

The anxiety of waiting for the dice to come to you, plus all the action around you can make you nervous to the point where you forget what you are about. You must develop that confidence that you are the man and you have the tools to succeed.

If taking that breathe before the toss helps you, then do it. It should be part of your memory bank and done without thinking. When you grip the dice breathe and throw.

Until you can come to the table with confidence, you will just be another contributor to the casino bottom line.

Chapter 11

Practice Makes Perfect

The Key to a good practice is practice often.

Back to the basics! Sometimes we tend to forget what is important when practicing. We tend to concentrate on the toss and forget about setting the dice. The more we set the dice, the more we get use to where the numbers are on the dice. The more we set the dice in our practice sessions the more familiar we become with the dice. Never leave home without them.

It's when I try a new set or permutation that I slow down on setting. Once I get 72 to 108 tosses in, my memory banks start to function and the new set becomes second nature.

How long should we practice and what should we be practicing on? Good question and one with several answers. You will need something to throw the dice onto, such as a homemade practice rig or box, pool table or a real casino table. Space and ingenuity will determine your options.

Once you have a practice option in place, you should start your early practice sessions with the grip and toss. Two to three hours a day for two to three weeks would be an excellent beginning. Then move into setting the dice by picking out a set from the recommended list of basic sets.

When I started out, I used the hard-way set to help determined how well I was doing. Which means you should start recording every toss from now on. If you change sets, start your recordings over. When I started, we didn't have "Bone Tracker." I recorded everything by hand (65,000+) throws. Bone Tracker has made things easier now.

Tossing, setting and recording went on for four or five months. I fell into a routine of practicing at least one hour a day after the first year. The second year I went down to a half hour a day. Now I try to get twenty minutes in when I can. I practice with variety of sets that I feel I will use at the Boat. I throw fifteen to twenty tosses just before leaving for the Boat.

A good way to practice is incorporate betting in with your grip, set and toss practice. Practice your betting strategies along with your tosses. If you practice on a felt layout, place a chip on each number you throw, including the sevens. This will give you an idea of what each set is doing for you.

The key to practice is to practice. How much you practice will be determined by how good you want to be. Make practicing fun. Invite a friend over to practice with you. Have contests to see who can throw the least amount of sevens etc.

Chapter 12

Part 1 - Table Longevity

Extending your play at the tables can be achieved by being prepared in advance.

Recently I was asked how I manage to keep my head above water while spending so much time at the boats. It got me to thinking about how we were successful when most of the players around us were losing. When losing, we seem to lose less than those around us.

Then there is the question of why we lose less, when everybody else is drowning. To survive in this game you have to be prepared to make changes in midstream. Your preparation before hand plays a big part in being successful more often than not.

In the last six weeks we have been to the boat four times. We have come out ahead twice and lost twice but our bottom line is on the plus side.

Being successful in craps doesn't mean you just won more than you lost. It depends on how you played the game. Are you prepared for this sport? Have you been working out? Are you prepared to make quick changes and react to the ever changing hot and cold tables? Preparation is the key. Just like all the other sports, you have to practice to gain the skills needed to help you be the last man standing at the table.

You have to learn to rely on your own skills as a shooter and be prepared to back off everybody else. Be alert for other players that show skills like your own, but give them time to prove themselves. No matter how skilled you become, you are not going to win every time you step up to the table.

When and if you become an advantage player, be careful of all your friends who are going to want to go to the casino and do what you do. My daughter is one of them. She started out using the pincer grip. Her last visit to Vegas I noticed she was using a two finger grip and setting the V-3. I asked her why she changed. She said I read your book.

Even my own father-in-law remarked that if he ever goes to a casino, he would only bet when I had the dice. I told him he probably would lose. It seems every time I am at the table with my daughter, I can't hit the broadside of the back wall.

Getting back to the longevity thing at the table, Laser and I have a few simple rules we follow. We will never play out of position. We consider SR and SL-1 and 2 are acceptable. We don't play beyond our stop loss. We will try and defuse any consternation at the table. We watch the reaction of each others toss. When Clubsodakenny is with us, he counts the tosses. We try to keep our crew at three and watch each other's back. We prefer $10 tables and old felt layouts. We practice. We also take into consideration the compatibility of the table crew and suits.

We know our weaknesses and know when to pull in our horns or in my case, when to back off the C&E's and get off the randy's. In Laser's case, he would back off the hard six's and twelve.

I often bring up Laser's name because he is a student of the game and the best student I have had the privilege of working with and now playing with. I worked with him for two months before we set foot on a boat casino. We did quite well for two guys learning and practicing on a pool table. Now we have been going first class and practicing on Clubsodakenny's twelve foot regulation table.

Table longevity can be achieved by being well prepared. You must have a game plan and be prepared to go to plan "B", depending on game conditions. The theme in my first and second book was "Wait and Fire." That holds true to this day, "Wait and Fire." "Wait." until the numbers are running and then "Fire." Good hunting......... and keep it simple.

Part 2 – Table Discipline

Surviving a full table of random shooters takes patience and discipline for the Dice Setter to have any chance at all to show a profit.

Let's look at a worst case real world reality scenario. We walk into our favorite casino or boat and find our favorite table filled up with random players called "Randies." While you are surveying the crap pit, you're position at SR1 opens up and you quickly jump into the spot.

Looking around the table, you don't recognize any players and realize you're at a round table of random shooters. The player next to you informs you that the person, who just left your spot, just had a nice run and colored up. Now it dawns on you that SL1 has the dice and you are going to have to wait on eleven randies to shoot before you get the dice. What to do?

You can start by fumbling around with your buy-in money and player's card. Don't drop it on the table till SL1 sevens out. The dealer may say go ahead and drop it on the table. Don't do it. After the seven-out, drop the money! One down, ten to go. Be slow in picking up your chips. Take your time organizing your chips in the rail. Wait for that next shooter to seven-out before you make a bet. Two down, nine to go.

The guy on the hook now has the dice. Wait till he has a point and then place the six or eight. Play out the six or eight or both as you normally would, till there is a seven- out. Three down, eight to go. Straight out (SO1) now has the dice. If the suits are sleeping, we will skip Mr. SO1 and not bet on him. Four down, seven to go. We will make our place bet on SO2. Five down, six to go.

We intended to skip play on the dealers hook left (DHL), but he showed signs of a consistent toss and was setting the dice. He made a point so we make a PL bet with odds and wait it out, unless he shows a lot of numbers. Six down, five to go. We will skip play on DHR. Seven down, four to go. SO2 gets a place bet. Eight down, three to go. We have to be careful with SO1 and take notice if the suits or box is watching our betting pattern as we get closer to our turn with the dice. If they are still sleeping, we won't bet on SO1. Nine down, two to go.

We will make a place bet on SR Hook and play it out. Ten down, one to go! We will make a PL bet with odds on SR2. What we did not anticipated was SR2 going on a tear and holding the dice for twenty minutes. Eleven down and it's our turn with the dice, finally. We make our PL bet, set the dice, make the toss and get six for the point.

You guess it. Point seven and out. Well, I told you it was a worst case scenario.

To do all this in real life, takes discipline and patience. Just remember that in craps nothing is written in stone. You have to be flexible and go with the flow. The above example can be switched around to meet a developing situation. When you're standing around not betting on a shooter, have some chips in your hand like you might be going to make a bet. Change your pattern of play. If you can get away with it, skip two or three players in a row. Don't be obvious about it. Look like your about to make a bet and then hold back.

Discipline is one of the key ingredients to being a successful Dice Influencer. Basics and Etiquette aside, the ability to execute patients and discipline is paramount to successful winning sessions.

Most people know the basics but do they know how to employ it? Few people practice good dice etiquette and it shows at the tables. Keeping your patience at the table is a must if you want to be a winner. **Let the game come to you. Don't chase the game**.

Chapter 13

Percent of Components Importance

Rating the necessary components of a good dice influencer can be difficult.

I believe the five skills, Discipline, Shooting skill, Betting strategy, bankroll and knowledge of the game are all equal in their importance to become an accomplished craps player.

DISCPLINE: 19%. Without it, your other skills are wasted. With it can mean the difference between a win and a loss.

SHOOTING SKILL: 19%. Means nothing if you don't have the other four skills. Without it, you are just another random roller.

BETTING STRATEGY: 19% it's the difference of winning big or little. You need a strategy to take advantage of the current trend.

BANKROLL: 19% if you are short stacked; you won't be able to take advantage of any good rolls. Without a sufficient bankroll, you will be playing scared.

KNOWLEDGE OF THE GAME: 19% if you don't know what you're doing, your other skills are useless. Knowledge of all aspects of the game maximizes your chances of winning.

ABILITY TO READ TABLE: 1.5% Most of the time we are stuck with whatever table is available.

TREND: 1.5% goes hand in hand with above. Soon or later the trend will become obvious.

TABLE KARMA: 1% we can only hope the table becomes friendly and the crew is okay.

LUCK 1% A precision shooter makes his own luck. You can't predict luck.

SUPERSTITION: 0% As far as I'm concerned, it doesn't come into play.

In conclusion, if any one of the top five is missing, you are in big trouble.

The bottom five, if you are LUCKY, you will have the ABILITY TO READ THE TABLE and determined the TREND and ignore any SUPERSTITIONS and enjoy the TABLE KARMA.

Chapter 14

Mental Status

What is your mental assessment of your position in the Dice Community?

For years there have been three basic groups of craps players. They are: **Gamblers, recreational players and professional players.** Just about everybody that plays craps will fall into one of these three groups.

Which category do you fit? Are you a **gambler**? Do you have to bet on every shooter? Do you play a lot of high risk bets? Do you play other table games or video poker without learning basic strategy? Do you bet on all sports, just to have action on the game while you are watching the game? Are you stopping at the casino, boat or OTB everyday to make some kind of bet? If you do, you're a "Gambler".

Another sign is when you are betting with money that is ear marked for essential things in your everyday living. If this is the case, you better consider calling that phone number that is posted on all the casino publicity material.

The second group you might fall into is the "**Recreational Player**". The recreational player could be someone that only plays when on vacation or on special occasions. It could be someone who just enjoys the game and has plenty of money he can afford to lose. He will make more bets than practical and doesn't mind the losses. These are usually the one's that go to Las Vegas once or twice a year and that is the only time they see the inside of a casino. They usually have no strategy or plan of what they want to accomplish at the table.

A Lot of your high rollers, known as whales, fall into this group. They just have too much money they don't know what to do with.

The third group encompasses the **"Professional Gambler"** or in our case the "Professional Craps Player". That's the player that makes a living shooting craps. There are not very many in this group. The few that I know all have other sources of income to fall back on. You could put those who qualify as instructors, sell dice products, hold seminars and write craps books in this category. Does that make them professional craps shooters? That's your call.

Because of the emergence of the dice setter we have the need for a new group. Call it the "The **Advantage Player**". This category would include the people who excel at influencing the dice and mastered a consistent set, grip and toss. Hopefully they would be schooled in dice etiquette and try to stay under the radar.

The Advantage Player cannot be compared to the Gambler because his skills are used only when he has the dice. When random rollers have the dice, he is usually on the side lines waiting for his turn or another AP to shoot. The AP could be a recreational player. The professional player would most certainly have to be an AP. The gambler may have the AP skills but invariably cancels them out when he bets on everybody and everything.

Where do you fit in? Where do I fit in? The question I hear the most, is why don't I play more often? You should go to the boat every night. I don't think so. I know my limitations. I am a conservative by nature and fit the recreational player group. We all have a little gamble in us. But I rule myself out of that group. I like to call it a hobby. I like to teach the game and help maintain the Website and write a book or four during the winter months when I can't participate in my other hobby, golf.

If you are going to be a dice setter, you must have the **proper mindset** to succeed. You must mentally know your limitations and where you fit into the Dice Community.

Good luck and good shooting, but not necessarily in that order.

Chapter 15

Etiquette

Craps Etiquette is a matter of common sense.

Common sense etiquette by the dice influencer will gain you respect from the table crew and suits. You're first appearance at the craps table will usually set the tone for that session. The first thing you should take into consideration is who has the dice and is he into a hot hand. You don't want to buy in during his roll especially if he is a random roller. That's one random roller you won't have to bet on.

If the box or dealer tell you to drop your buy-in on the table between tosses, tell him that's OK, you will wait till the shooter completes his hand and you don't want to jinx him. **That's Rule number 1; don't buy in till the shooter sevens-out.**

When you buy chips, buy in for your allotted amount for that session. Don't piece meal you buy-in like $100 at a time. If your bankroll for that session is $300, buy in for $300. Additional buy-ins only slows down play. The larger your buy-in, the higher you're rating will be. The pit critters might miss your additional chip buys. **Rule number 2; don't slow down play by constantly buying small amounts of chips.**

When you're not shooting, keep you hands outside the rail and not hanging over the chip rack in the playing area. If you are leaning on the rail with your elbows, watch your head or you might be wearing the dice as glasses. That is **Rule number 3; Watch your hands.**

Late betting is the main cause for hands getting hit by the dice. Make sure you bet early enough to avoid getting hit by the dice. Throwing proposition bets on the table at the last second should be avoided. Plan in advance what bets you want in play. Tossing out a last second bet when the shooter has the dice can ruin his concentration especially if he or she is a DI. That's **Rule number 4; don't make late bets.**

Always give consideration the Shooter no matter who he is. When the shooter is next to you and ready to throw, step back and give him plenty of room to do his thing. It's also courteous to show him some encouragement by making a pass-line bet and not playing the DP. **Rule number 5; Shooting courtesy.** Keep unnecessary chatter to a minimum, especially when the shooter has the dice. Don't talk dice control at the table. Above all don't refer to anybody by their web site handles. **Rule number 6; Table chatter.**

A little friendliness towards the suits at the beginning of a session could pay dividends later on. When the suit or box person gives you back your player's card and wishes you good luck, you might remark that you like his tie. This usually gets things off on a good note. When the suit throws your card across the table and it almost takes your finger off, beware. He is usually a lazy type and not too interested in being friendly. If he walks around the table and comes out of the pit to return your card, he's a friendly type. **Rule number 7; be nice to the Suits.**

When to tip can be done in several ways. Playing a hard way or other prop bets is one way to tip the dealers. Some will tip when they leave the table. Others tip here and there when they feel like it. I like to tip when it's beneficial to me and the crew will notice. I only tip when I have the dice. I will put a white chip along side my PL bet. I make this bet for the crew every time I come out. If you throw some sevens and make a few points, the crew loves you and you will never hear a peep about the back wall. It doesn't make sense to tip when leaving the table. What good does it do you then? You're gone. **Rule number 8; tip when you will be recognized for it.**

Avoid any arguments with the crew or suits or anybody else at the table. Rather than ague, color up and get out of Dodge, **Rule number 9; avoid all consternations.**

When coloring up, be sure to wait for a proper opening in play before placing all your chips in front of you on the table. Announce color coming in and wait for the crew to direct you. There is nothing worse that three or four people coloring up at one time and you have the dice. Keep cool and try to avoid all the land mines. **Rule number 10; be patient when coloring up.**

There you have it. The ten commandments of Craps Etiquette!

Some additional thoughts on etiquette during casino play.

When playing straight out, keep you're PL and odds bet away from the shooter's landing area. Discreetly ask others at your end to do the same. If you are the shooter, don't yell down the table for someone to move his or her chips. That would only bring more attention to you. If there is no one to help you out, just try to avoid the land mines as best as you can.

Chapter 16

Heat or Retreat

Can you take the heat or do you make a fast retreat.

First off, what is **"HEAT"** pertaining to craps? Heat is an aggravation provided by an over zealous pit critter in a suit. It could come from a pit boss with tunnel vision thinking he is preventing the casino from going bankrupt. It most likely will come from a vermin called a floor manager who will spend his time drinking coffee and standing behind the box person making notations on your file card charting your action.

HEAT could come from a bored box person who doesn't like your looks and is trying to get promoted to drinking coffee. Once in a while a dealer who needs a refresher course in customer relations will get on your case because you had to correct him too many times on payouts. The stick person can be a thorn in your side when he or she starts flashing that sword around and mixing up the dice so you can't pick out your numbers fast enough when setting. They like to fish with that stick, but the only thing they are catching is your scorn.

That's quite an army you are up against. You might have three Suits, couple box persons, a crew of four rotating in and out. It's you against the house and their house is a big fort. What can you do to even out the odds against you? You can start by being nice and friendly. It may be hard to do when the Suit fires your player's card back at you and almost takes your finger off when you are picking up you chips. A good Suit will come around the outside of the table and hand you your card by name and wish you good luck. Sometimes even the box or dealer will wish you good luck when you receive your buy-in chips. This is the sign of a friendly table.

When the dealer says, "Oh no, not another dot-com guy", you know you got trouble. Be ready to RETREAT. He might say, "Let's see if this guy can hit the back wall." I love it when they ask me how long it took me to learn to throw the dice that way. I tell them ten years and I still have a long way to go. One guy asked me if I knew FS and said that I shoot just like him. I came back with, am I really that bad? They laughed and the situation was defused.

The minute you throw the dice, they know what you're up to and will be keeping an eye on you. Get use to it and be friendly. Their best recourse is to harp on hitting the back wall. Some day they will wake up and realize that's what we are trying to do. Some of the smarter Suits are turning their backs on one die missing the back wall. After all, it's a random roll.

Most of your random rollers are setting the dice in some form or other. They look for their favorite number to put on top and then just fire them down the table. Some of them are very meticulous on what they are setting and then shake the hell out of the dice before tossing. All these habits of the random rollers only serve to help us blend in.

Some time when you think the Suit is hanging around to see if you are one of those "dot com" guys, try this. When it's your turn to throw the dice, just pick them up without setting them but make your fine smooth delivery to the back wall with both dice. The suit will think you have a nice toss but you're not setting the cubes and he might just walk away and go for another cup of coffee. Sometimes it pays to sacrifice that first come-out roll.

Be careful of that first bet you make for the crew. I have a habit of making a PL bet right off the bat on my come-out roll. If you don't know the crew or suit, it's a sure tip off to them that you're up to something. If I don't know the Suit I will wait a couple of tosses before putting out a bet for them. When putting out bets for the crew, look at it as buying an insurance policy. I am a firm believer in betting for the crew only when I have the dice.

We are our own worst enemy when it comes to drawing heat. We may be throwing the dice too high or to low or too hard. We may be taking too much time setting the dice. We might be placing our bets too late. Not hitting the back wall is their favorite ploy against us. It is up to us to determine what real heat is and what appears as routine banter. The minute we take up arguing with any of the crew or suits, we will get the worst of it.

Nothing has changed over the years. The same kind of heat was being applied ten years ago. Sometimes for no apparent reason the casino would apply heat. Fifty Roller and I were exposed to the heat, ten years ago, at the Casino Royale. What happened to us is happening all over when you run into an over zealous pit critter. We were at a $2 table, with 100Xodds. We had bought in for $300 each. Nothing much was happening until Fifty Roller got the dice. We were not into dice setting at that time and were just making the rounds. As soon as Fifty Roller picked up the dice the Suit came over and whispered something into the box guy's ear. On the next toss the Suit again whispered something to the box guy. Fifty Roller was about to throw again when the box guy says," let's hit the back wall with both dice. He had a pained expression on his face like he didn't want to say anything.

Fifty Roller was ignoring what was going on and throwing some numbers. In the process he made a couple of points and the Suit went nuts. He pulled the box guy out and sat down at the box. Before he could say anything Fifty Roller seven's out.

I got the dice next and before I could toss them, the" Suit-in-the-box" says, "make sure you hit the back wall with the dice." I whispered to Fifty Roller to make his best play and when I seven-out, we retreat to the high ground next door.

The Suit kept baiting me and I was just trying to finish the hand and retreat. When I think back on the session, I tried to think what got the Suit so uptight or worried about us. Was it the $300 buy-in at a $2 table or the $5 bets inside and stacking all the winnings on the pass line odds on the point of six? I made the six and went point seven and out.

As soon as I seven-out, the Suit got up and let the box guy sit back down. As we retreated from the table, the box guy said, "sorry about that."

We proved one point. You don't have to be a dice setter to attract attention. We were random rollers with stylish tosses and caught enough heat to have to retreat.

Is, *"Hit the Back Wall,"* Really Heat?

Going back as far as I can remember some forty five years, the casino craps personnel have been warning players to hit the back wall. Some times I think it is an automatic reaction to any throw that misses the back wall.

I remember one time when I missed the back wall with one die and the dealer in a bored monotone says, "You have to hit the back wall." The stick guy came right back with, "Wake up, this guy has been playing for two hours and hasn't missed the back wall till now."

Another time in a downtown casino where I swear the table was only a ten footer, I missed the back wall while trying to adjust to the short toss. This older stickman says, "Try and hit the back wall sir". After my next toss the stickman whispers to me, "thanks for hitting the back wall".

I wouldn't consider either one of these occurrences "heat." Heat is when they, the table crew or pit vipers add a remark to the back wall warning, such as, "or you will have to pass the dice". That's the start or real heat.

Most of the time they are just doing their job! They have been programmed by the suits. If it doesn't pertain to me, I don't worry about it.

Chapter 17

Money Management

Money Management or how can I keep what I got and still enjoy the thrill of playing the game of craps?

We saw in **Chapter 4** that we must eliminate the practice of playing with scared money. We exposed you to betting a minimal amount on the ten Random rollers at your table. This style of play lets you bet on all of the random rollers at the table allowing a minimum one unit bet on each. This is a worst case scenario and should be treated as a way to bring this table of ten down to a manageable number of players with less risk to your bankroll.

If there are ten RR's at the table and you are at a $10 table and you may bet one unit on the RR if your buy-in was $400. You have $200 to bet on the RR's and $200 to bet on yourself. Let's look at the single unit bet on the RR's. We will call it our "Bet-em-all" style of play. I would bet $12 on the place eight. If Randy sevens out, you will lose $12! If eight RR's seven out without tossing an eight, you are out $96. In this worst case scenario, you would back off betting the last two RR's.

This style of betting will have you on a Randy, if he should

get into a hot roll. Any kind of hot roll will have some six and eights and you hope to be on one or the other when it happens.

Now you have the dice and $50 allocated to your turn. I would make a $10 pass line bet with single odds and $12 placed on the six and eight and a $6 C&E bet. The C&E bet is not recommended for novice players. You don't have to bet the entire $50 on your turn. You might opt to just play the pass line with single odds.

With this type of allocation of funds you will be able to make at least two complete rounds and two turns with the dice. If you are not seeing any light at the end of the tunnel, it's time to apply your stop loss at $300 or a figure of your choosing.

The expectancy of the eight showing every 7.2 tosses will come into play in a random game. How you play the eight when it hits is up to you. You have the option of coming down with a profit of $14 and you have just eliminated one Randy and gained a free ride on the next one.

Another option is to spread to the six if you feel the shooter has any ability. You can just stay up and go for a second hit. Any time you can eliminate a randy without making a bet is good money management. Remember, this is a worst case scenario and we must try to eliminate betting on as many RR's as possible.

Some sessions will turn into everybody throwing sevens and you may be faced with some of the worst players in the world. That is why we must try to avoid as many RR's as possible. If you feel you have to have action, try betting on just every other one. This eliminates half the field. If you have a place bet on a Randy and he throws like a jerk, pull your bet down. The dealer will have noticed that you made a bet on the guy to start out with. Look for the least little thing to not bet or take your bet down. If you don't like his looks, don't bet him.

The Suits are more interested in what the shooter is doing and won't be too interested in what you are doing. If you have been standing around and not betting, the Suits or box person might tell the stick person to by-pass you.

If the guy to your right has a hot roll, you might start yelling for everybody to pass the dice back to him. You're going to get the dice next anyhow and you want to avoid that quick seven-out that usually follows a good hand.

If a shooter is setting the dice and has a nice toss, jump on him and skip the next shooter. On your place bet, try using the reverse five count. If you haven't got a hit on the forth fifth toss, pull your place bet down. Make sure you make a pass-line bet when the player on your right has the dice. All these little maneuvers will help you preserve your bankroll till you can get your hands on the dice. Then it's show time.

The Fifty-Fifty Play

Here's something you can try to discipline yourself on managing your play. For example if you buy in for $400, put $200 in your front chip rack and $200 in the back chip rack. Do your betting out of the front rack and put 50% of your winnings in the back rack.

If you bet $12 to place on the eight and it hits, put $7 in the front rack and $7 in the back rack. This way you will be contributing to your retirement fund while increasing your total amount of chips available for betting. Remember what goes in the back rack, stays in the back rack. If you lose the chips in the front rack, you are done for that session. It's called managing your money.

Game With In a Game

The game with in a game is a favorite of mine. All you have to do is put out a C&E or horn bet along with your pass line bet on the come-out. Set for the eleven on two sides of the dice or use the straight sixes set.

The second part of the play takes over after you set a point. It's that simple! If you are at a $10 table you could put $6 on the C&E and if a 2, 3, or 12 would be thrown, you win $18. If the eleven comes up you win $42. If a seven shows you still win $4. If you set a point you are into the second game.

Front End Loading

Sometimes you have to be hit on the head, before you wake up to what's going on around you when it comes to betting in craps. We have been brain wash to waiting for the hot hand to come around. We have been told to do the "five count" on everybody or wait till the shooter has thrown a few times before making a bet.

A craps education is in order for those who wish to become dice influencers. The fact is the random roller is expect to throw a seven every six tosses. More realistic is they won't have over four tosses before the seven shows. Why then would we want to wait to later in the roll to make a bet?

One of the dice community's best writers and by far the most knowledgeable is the Mad Professor who has put out extensive material on the subject. His writings can be found at the Dice Institute.com.

The theory goes that if the seven is expected to show within six tosses of the dice, we should put more money on the early tosses before the seven is expected. That means loading up on the front end of the roll with larger bets. It means putting up a larger bet for the first four rolls and then backing down as the roll proceeds.

If you bet $30 on the eight and hit during the first four tosses you can change your bet to a $12 eight and pocket $23. You could also expand to a $12 six and still pocket $11. The idea is to load up on the front end then regress or even come down. Save it for another day or roll.

Chapter 18

Betting Strategy – To Come or Place

One of the most frequent questions I get from beginners and friends alike, is do you play the COME bet? My answer is simple, NO! Then they ask, why? This section is dedicated to those individuals who want to learn a common sense way of approaching the game of craps when it comes to **COME or PLACE betting.**

For years my colleges have been writing books that 90% of them advocate one simple basic strategy. That was to make a PASS LINE bet and take full odds, make two COME bets and take full odds. That was it. When you were winning, they suggested you make another COME bet or cover the six or eight if not already cover. For years I played this way.

Back in the early nineties, the world's greatest self proclaimed gambling writer came up with the "five count." I tried it. I even wrote about it in my first book. I suggested some refinements to get away from the "Dewy, Don't" system. While doing my research on the first book I finally woke up to the fact that the come-bet and the place-bet were pretty much alike in pay offs at lower X-odds but there were several interesting observation to be considered.

I will use Las Vegas Strip X odds 3, 4, 5 for comparison.

After the point is established the COME bet and PLACE bet come into play. You bet $5 on the COME. The shooter throws a six and the dealer puts your $5 in the box with the big number six in it. I already have PLACED the six for $30 and collected $35. The shooter then throws another six. You have taken full odds X5, $25 which is a total $30. We both collect $35. Who made the best bet? The PLACE better of course.

When you PLACE bet, you only need one hit to collect. The come better needs two hits to collect. The PLACE better gets 7 to 6 odds, 5 X 7 =$35. The COME better gets 6 to 5 odds, 5 X 6 + $5 = $35. The odds are a wash.

One good point about the COME bet is you have 8 chances in 36 of the shooter throwing a 7 or 11 on the come-out for a winner and only 4 chances in 36 of the losing 2, 3, or 12 coming up.

Another drawback to consider is what occurs on the come-out roll. When that come-out seven pops up and you have two or three come bets established, those bets are working contract bets and are losers to the come-out seven. Traditionally, come-out bet odds are not working on a come-out roll (unless you ask the dealer to have them "working"), so the odds portion of your bets are returned to you, but you do lose the flat portion of your original come bets. At this stage, all your bets are down and you have to start setting up come bets all over again.

When you do win a come bet, if you don't have another bet in the COME area, your bet and winnings are returned to you and your bet is down.

On the other hand your PLACE bets will stand forever until the seven shows. You have the freedom of choosing any box number you want and you can press at any time. You can press the free-odds portion of the come bet at any time until you reach the table maximum for the free odds. Also, many, if not most, casinos will allow you to increase the flat portion of the original come-bet in order to increase amount of free odds to the next level.

What does all this mean to the dice setter or random roller? **The dice setter will make bets that will enhance his results based on his signature numbers.** The random players will get a faster return on their bets. The main concern is to get your original investment back in your chip rack as fast as possible.

This is just a common sense strategy to help the dice setter become a better advantage player by concentrating on his strengths.

Chapter 19

Don't Pass, Don't Come, Don't Play!

To become a fully rounded player, it is necessary to know the pros and cons of playing the **DON"T PASS LINE and the DON"T COME BOX.**

Don't players, some times known as **"Wrong Players"** and **"Dark Side Players"** are a minority group of players. They are usually quiet and very often pass the dice.

You can usually spot a "Don't player at the dealers hook so he can be close to that Don't Come box on the layout. Players that play the "Don't," are sometimes referred to as playing the dark side. I guess it is because they seem to put a dark cloud over a table of enthusiastic players. Here is a play on words! If the "Don't" player is considered a "Wrong" better by betting on the seven to show, then the players betting that the seven doesn't show, must be the "Right Players".

When we run into a cold table, the first reaction is to jump on the "Dark Side." A couple come-out sevens soon discourage that. How could that happen to us on a cold table? Mathematics my friend! The felt always looks greener on the other side of the table.

Let's look at what is happening. Both the Pass Line and the Don't Pass Line pay even money. What are the expectations of each bet? Looking for a PL winner, we have 8 chances in 36 to win our PL bet or 4.5 to 1. The expectations of the DP winning on the come-out are 3 chances in 36 or 12 to 1. That's a pretty steep wall to climb to get on board with a DP bet.

Now let's look at the behind the line odds bet. At a $5 table we have $5 on the PL and take single odds of $5 for a total of $10 at risk. The point is ten. The Darksider puts $5 on the DP and takes $10 odds for a total of $15 at risk. For his $15 risk, he can win $10. For our $10 at risk, we can win $15. The point of ten pays the right better 2 to 1 odds and pays the wrong better 1 to 2 odds. I guess we know why they call "Don't" betters "Wrong" betters.

Once the point is established we have a new set of expectations. An expectation of winning ten as the point is 1 chance in 12. The "Don't" better has 1 chance in 6. What the "Don't" player has to decide is if you want to take the risk of the opening come-out, verses the advantage you pick up after the point is established.

All expectations are based on the 36 possible results on the toss of a pair of dice. The question you have to consider is whether the 33 expectations of keeping your PL bet in play outweighs the 28 expectations of the DP bet being kept alive. It's obvious that the PL bet has the advantage on the come out.

With a point established and the DP player bet is still alive, he has 6 expectations out of 36 to win his bet or 33, 32, or 31 possibilities of keeping his bet alive, depending on the point. The PL better will have 30 possibilities of staying alive, no matter what the point is. The best case scenario for the DP better is for the point to be four or ten.

The advantage the PL play has over the DP play on the come-out, out weighs the advantage the DP gains after the point is established. It's a close call, but when you are in doubt about what to do at a choppy or cold table, play the expectation game.

The **"Don't Come"** bet expectations are the same as the PL and DP expectations. Your odd's bet will be the reverse of the come bet. For a six or eight DC bet, you would have to bet $6 to win $5. For the five and nine you would have to bet $6 to win $4. For the four and ten you would have to bet $6 to win $3.

In my simplistic way of thinking, why would you want to bet more to win less when you can bet less to win more? Taking odds on "Don't" bets can be hazardous to your bankroll. When I go on tilt on a really cold table, I will bet more straight up on the DP and take no odds. A win will get me even money. If I took odds I would receive less then even money for what I invested or put at risk.

A good dice influencer can change the odds into his favor, no matter what side he plays on. If you have the dice you can change that cold table to your advantage. When someone else has the dice you are at their mercy and you would do good to heed the expectation game.

The great full time gambler, "Nick the Greek" mostly played the dark side. He died broke.

Chapter 20

Playing the Six and Eight on Randies

The question I get the most these days is, "How do you play the random rollers?" The best answer is don't play them. We all know that is almost impossible. We may travel many miles to play once or twice a month and when we get there we don't feel like standing around waiting for the dice to come around. The smart thing to do is avoid as many random rollers as possible.

To do this, you can only go to the men's room so often. When a RR is coming out you could try and engage someone behind you in conversation so as to miss making a pass line bet and then wait for the next shooter. If you are with friends, have one of them call you on your cell phone. Step back and give a quick answer get back at the table and wait for the hand to finish. Then ask for a towel to put over your chips and say that you have to make a call. You can stay away from the table a lot longer with this ploy. You want to check on where the dice are every so often. You can do this by walking by the table with the cell phone pressed against your ear.

Asking for a chair can also give you some stalling time. The thing is I didn't come to the casino to stand around with my hands in my pocket, spending my time in the men's room, talking with someone, talking on a cell phone or waiting for a chair.

What is the alterative? How about playing the numbers game or better yet playing the expectation game. We all know that the seven is expected to show up within six tosses. We also know that the six and eight together, one of them is expected to show in four tosses. The six and eight together are a powerful combination to be reckoned with. We are talking about playing random rollers with the best expectancy numbers.

Expectancy tosses is what random rollers are all about. If you bet the six and eight together and you don't hit one of them, get out of Dodge. Turn off your bet or take them down. If you do get a hit, consider coming down. If you get a hit right off the bat, consider staying up for three more tosses. If you get that second hit you have options. You can press, collect or come down and wait for the next shooter.

I love playing six and or eights on RR's. Some times I will just play the eight on them. If it hits, I can press, spread to the six or come down depending if I like the looks of the shooter. Remember, the key to good money management is to get your investment off the table ASAP and play with the casino's chips.

It's very important to know the expectations of every random toss. There are 36 possible outcomes on a randomly thrown pair of dice. In 36 tosses, the seven is expected to show six times. The six and eight each are each expected to show five times. Bet together, they are expected to show ten times as compared to six times for the seven. That makes the six and eight a very powerful pair. It's the best deal in town and even gets better when you or a DI has the dice and you set for the six and eight for the point. You place the eight and on the next roll or two he throws an eight. Then he throws a five and you make a Field bet. He throws a twelve and you get paid triple and rack the winnings. Mr. Randy then throws another eight, so you place the six. If he throws another five, six or eight on the next toss, you jump back on the field (one unit). He throws an eleven and you hear the thunder overhead.

You are now set to take that Field money and press the six and eight or expand to the five and nine. That's being in sync with the game at hand, no matter who has the dice. You have at least five units in the rack and ready for lightning to strike. From this point on I would press one unit on each hit. As soon as I had three or four units on the five, six and eight, I would set up the iron cross with a one unit Field bet.

Would I take my bets down or regress at any point? No. We skimped and scraped to get this far and are set up to shake the money tree.

Being out of sync is when you watch the next Randy throw three sevens on the come-out and you are standing their with your chips in your hand. Then you watch him throw two six's and an eight, so you place the six and eight.

Randy then seven's out on the next toss. You are out of sync. Call it luck or bad luck; it's still a guessing game with the Randy's.

Now when the dice setter has the dice, it's a new ball game of expectation. How do you know when you're in that hot hand? Don't worry, you will know. After seven or eight rolls you will gain more and more confidence. Confidence and concentration takes over and you only think about the next toss.

That's why I don't watch the clock or count tosses when I have the dice. After I place my bets, I'm only interested in how the stick person is presenting me with the dice. Next I concentrate on the set and then the toss. The last thing I do before the toss is to glance at the dice alignment with the back wall.

How you set the dice is determined by what is working for you at that particular table. In my recent trip to Vegas, I set the 3-V 90% of the time. During the three one hour plus rolls, I got the feeling that I would never throw a seven. There is no better feeling than to have the dice in a monster roll with the whole table yelling and screaming for that hard eight and you throw it.

Having the crew on your side also helps. It also helps when two of the stick persons set the dice for you. They were not only giving me the dice with the three's on top, but had the six and two facing me the way I wanted it. One dealer coming back from break said, "Does he still have the dice?"

When it was all over the Floor Manager said, "Nice hand, congratulations". I should mention that tipping is a must. That brings the crew into the game.

Discipline is the name of the game. If you have to play a Randy, make sure you play the minimum on the numbers that gives you the best random expectation of winning.

Chapter 21

Playing the Iron Cross

Simply put, the Iron Cross can be a beautiful tool to add to your arsenal. Other players will watch you with envy while you collect on every throw of the dice.

"The Iron Cross" is one of my favorite betting strategies. It's a play that should be worked into gradually and should be used only sparingly on random rollers. It's very useful when another advantage player has the dice and is throwing nothing but "field" numbers. How many times have you been at the table where you keep throwing "field" numbers till you can't stand it and throw out a field bet out of frustration? Been there and done that!

Let's go over the semantics on betting the **"Iron Cross"**. First of all I equate the word "Iron" as meaning strong play when it is properly put into place. The "Cross" is what the bets look like when in place. This may be stretching it a bit but you will get the idea. The objective of the play is to have bets on the 5, 6, 8 and "field". That puts you in position to gain a win no matter what number is thrown as long as it is not a SEVEN. If the seven shows, you lose all four bets. That's the down side of the play What we have to do is work our way into the **"Iron Cross"** set up. There will be times when your normal play will put you in position to move quickly into the "Cross" bets. One example is when you have the dice and have just established the point of five. My automatic play would be to take double odds behind the pass line. (We will use a $10 minimum table in all examples.) Then I would place the six and eight for $12 each. This is a standard move by a lot of players. Now I can set back and wait for a couple hits or even make my point. When I feel comfortable getting about most of my initial bet of $54 off the table, I would consider pressing the six and eight up one unit to $18 each. One more hit and I would press one more unit on the six and eight to $24 each. At this point I'm thinking "Iron Cross". I would then make a $10 "field" bet. The "Iron Cross" is set.

One more hit and I am a happy camper. I would press the six and eight up to $30 each. I have $30 on the point of five and I will try to remember to keep the $10 "field" bet on board. My goal is to maintain $30 on the six and eight, $25 on the five and double odds on what ever ends up the point. At this point of the game if the seven shows, I should be close to even or ahead.

I love it when 5, 6, or 8 is the point. There is always the chance that you can work into the **"iron Cross"** slowly by just letting the game come to you.

Suppose you are playing just the six and eight place bets and a fellow DI has ten for the point. You might of pressed upward a couple of times and have your initial $24 bet back in your rack.

It's time to think about throwing a place bet on the five and forget about the ten. If the DI is setting the V2, there could be a lot of "field" numbers coming up and you want to be ready to take advantage of it.

Sometimes I will just place the eight on RR's. If the RR throws a quick eight, I might tell the dealer, give me a six.

A couple hits and we go to work after we get our $12 off the board.

The **"Iron Cross"** is a beautiful money tree when you get into a nice run. You can harvest a good crop of chips when those "field" numbers start to grow. Keep in mind that you can get burned up if the seven shows up early in the roll. Once you are set up and nothing but 5, 6 and 8's are hitting, get off the "field" bet in a hurry.

If you are in a really long roll, you can press upward one unit on each number as the hit. Just make sure you put that green chip in your rack. You will be surprised how you can turn a negative session into a profitable one by using a little common since. Stay alert. Nothing is more aggravating than to forget to replace your "field" bet and a twelve or two comes up and you miss a double payout. You might tell the stick to remind you of your field bet.

When setting up and playing the **"Iron Cross"**, take it slow and easy and let the "Cross" come to you. There will be sessions where you won't get a chance to set it up on the cheap. Setting it up before you bailed out your seed money is suicide.

Chapter 22

Regressing Your Bets

Regressing your bet's main purpose is to remove your capital in jeopardy, but still have some chips in play.

Regressing my bets? I very rarely regress my bets. When I do, I will bet the inside numbers and when they get one or two hits, I would regress down to the two unit stage. Example: At a 2 unit, $10 table I would bet $25 on the 5 and 9 and $30 on the 6 and 8. If the point is one of the inside numbers, I would put $20 in odds behind the $10 Pass Line bet. That's $110 inside and in jeopardy. If I regress to two units after one hit, I now have $44 in play and only $9 in jeopardy.

A second hit puts $14 in my rack for a $5 profit, none of my money is at risk and I have four numbers working. From this point on I have options. I can press each number as it hits and show a $2 profit on a one unit press. Repeat hits on the same number calls for a one unit press. When I am back up to $25 or $30's on my inside numbers, I would only bet $10 presses and bank $25 on each hit from then on.

I prefer to work with three numbers or less and when I have my money off the board I would press only one unit at a time. The secret to good money management is to always put 50% or more from each winning hit in your rack.

The hardest thing to do in this game is to say, "Take me down." When you have been in a hot roll for awhile and you have four or five numbers loaded up, how many hits is it going to take to equal what you have on the board? Listen to that little guy in your head and call all your bets off. That's another $110 or more profit you can put in the bank.

Try this simple way to see how you would fair during three sequences of rolls. The first using white chips and ending with a seven out after eight tosses. The next roll I used red chips and went seven out after ten tosses. The green chips represent sixteen tosses before the seven out. By looking at the results you can get an idea of how regressing your bets would have worked out. I threw two more tosses to round out a 36 toss session. The three seven outs resulted in a SRR of 12 for the session. Three sequences of tosses are not really enough but you will get the idea of what to expect.

The practice routine will help show you that elusive signature number that has a way of changing on you.

Chapter 23

Recognizing a Hot Hand

Recognizing a hot hand is the next step in your continuing search for a well rounded advantage in dice setting.

It's like looking for where lightning will strike next. Whether a random roller or you have the dice, it takes experience and sometimes just being **in sync with the game** at hand to become successful.

Being in sync with the game is making the right moves at the right time. For instance, you walk up to the table and buy in and a Randy throws four for the point. You place the eight and on the next roll or two he throws an eight. Then he throws a five and you make a Field bet. He throws a twelve and you get paid triple and rack the winnings. Mr. Randy then throws another eight, so you place the six. If he throws another five, six or eight on the next toss, you jump back on the field with a one unit bet. He throws a two or twelve and you hear the thunder overhead.

You are now set to take that Field money and press the six and eight or expand to the five and nine. That's being in sync with the game at hand, no matter who has the dice. You have at least five units in the rack and ready for lightning to strike. From this point on I would press one unit on each hit. As soon as I had three or four units on the five, six and eight, I would set up the iron cross, wit a one unit Field bet)

Would I take my bets down or regress at any point? No. We skimped and scraped to get this far and are set up to shake the money tree.

Being out of sync is when you watch the next Randy throw three sevens on the come-out and you are standing their with your chips in your hand. Then you watch him throw two six's and an eight, so you place the six and eight. Randy then seven's out on the next toss. You are out of sync. Call it luck or bad luck; it's still a guessing game with the Randy's.

Now when the dice setter has the dice, it's a new ball game of expectation. How do you know when you're in that hot hand? Don't worry, you will know. After seven or eight rolls you will gain more and more confidence. Confidence and concentration takes over and you only think about the next toss.

There are other **signs of hot hands** in progress or developing. A crowded table with a lot of cheering going on is a sure bet something exciting is taking place. The problem is the table is so crowded that you can't get close enough to see what's going on let alone make a bet.

When the roll is over the smart players will color up and head for the cashiers cage. The not so smart players will continue to play and give back what they won.

Be very careful when moving into your position if it should become open right after a hot hand. It came open for a reason. The player leaving your position may have been the shooter and now you have to wait for the dice to come all the way around the table before you can shoot. Don't be in a rush to jump into a table that has just had a big run.

When checking out other tables that are quiet look at every ones chip rail. Does everyone have a lot of chips? This could be a sign of a consistently favorable table. Beware if the don't players are the only ones with a rack full of chips.

Then there are the tables that are half full of players. Laser910 put it best when inquiring if the table was cold. The stick guy said, "Very cold." Laser910 comes right back with, "Well, lets see if we can warm things up." A positive attitude is a must to be successful in this game and Laser910 has that positive attitude.

Hot and cold running tables are a random thing. We can only hope that we can develop the skill to influence the out come when we have the dice to produce staying power to prolong the life of our own hot run.

Chapter 24

Buy Bets and Lay Bets

What are Buy Bets and Lay Bets? **LAY BETS** are another way for the casinos to get you to bet more on each shooter on the assumption that you will be attracted by a full odds payout for a 5% assessment.

Part 1 - The Buy Bet

A **"Buy Bet"** is a bet you have to pay a fee for the privilege of making the play. Usually the four and ten are the only box numbers that attract this type of action. With the buy bet you are betting that the shooter or you will make the point.

There are times when a player, or even yourself, will notice fours or tens are showing up more than expected. Instead of placing the four or ten for $25 and receiving 9 to 5 for a potential $45 pay out, you can tell the dealer to buy the four or ten and toss him a green chip. If you win the bet you will be paid full 2 to 1 odds, minus your $1 fee for a $49 win.

The casinos will not charge you if you lose the bet.

If you want to buy more than the $25 on the four and ten, you can sometimes push the casinos to let you buy $20 up to $39 for the $1 fee. Usually the $1 fee goes up $1 for each $25 you buy.

Players sometimes buy the five and nine, but it is only worthwhile at higher bet amounts. The four and ten should always be bought if it is going to be played.

Is the buy bet worth while? If you are a type person who likes to throw manhole covers around or you are a strong dice influencer you can take your chances at throwing four or tens at three chances in thirty-six. Not for me! You can take your buy bet down at any time.

Part 2 - The Lay Bet

"Lay Bets" are much the same as the buy bet. The difference is you can bet that a seven will show before a particular number. Instead of placing numbers to win, you can "Lay" box numbers to lose.

Say you lay the four and ten and the shooter throws a four. You lose the four. You still have the ten working but if the shooter Seven's out, you win on the ten.

If the shooter throws a "Lay" box number, that number loses. If the shooter throws a seven, all laid box numbers win. The object of this play is to receive true odds on your winnings, minus commission.

Just like the "Buy" bet, it will cost you a 5% commission when you win. Different areas might want the 5% up front.

You can take any or all "Lay" bets down at any time. You also have the option to turn off all your box number bets at any time. "Turn my box number bets off", means your bets will stay on the layout but will have no action until you tell the dealer to turn your bets back on.

Your turnoff action will be indicated by a little button with "off" marked on it. The dealer will place the off button on your box bets and periodically ask if you want to remain off. This type of play is a guessing game and can be hazardous to your bankroll.

Chapter 25

Gimmick Bets

The gimmick bets are starting to take over the top of the proposition area and is causing a layout overload for the casino.

The gimmick bets are just that. They are a gimmick to get you to put more money on the table. Picture how the area in front of the box person would look. You could end up with, "Four Rolls No Seven, The Fire Bet, Hop Bets, All Bet, Small-Tall, High-Low and now they talking about bringing out a version of making all the numbers during your roll including the come-out rolls.

Part 1 - Four Rolls No Seven

Starting on the come-out roll, if you throw four times without throwing a seven, you win even money. That's it! Bet $25, win $25. Bets start at whatever the casino decide to set as a minimum. If it is a $5 table you will most likely have to bet at least a $5 minimum. The maximum is what the casino decides.

Advantage players should have a field day with this bet. I tried it for one session and won three out of four tries

Part 2 – High-Low

Layout space is in such demand that they had to dump the Big 6&8 from the corner it has held for years. This was to make room for their "High-Low" gizmo game. Simply put, all you have to do is pace a bet on the High (8, 9, 10, 11) or Low (3, 4, 5, 6) and if one of your selected group of numbers is thrown, you win even money. You also can bet the two or twelve and it will pay 5 for 1. It's a one roll bet.

Looking at the downside of the bet we see that a bet on the High or Low would have 14 expected chances to win and 22 expected losing results. The odds are 11 to 7 you will lose the bet.

Part 3 – All Bet

Simplicity is the only good side to this bet. All you have to do is throw all the numbers 2, 3, 4, 5, 6, 8, 9, 10, 11 and 12 before you seven-out. IF you do it, you will receive175 for 1.

Part 4 – All, Tall, Small Bet

If you can toss 2, 3, 4, 5, 6 before throwing a seven you win. If you toss 8, 9, 10, 11, 12 before a seven you win. Win the Small or the Tall; you will be paid 35 for 1. All will pay 175 to 1. A $3 bet on all three; ($1 on each) will pay $245.

Part 5 -- BIG 6&8

The BIG 6 &8 is slowly being fazed out of the game and being replaced by the High-Low bet. I haven't seen anyone play those corner bets very often. The casino will keep trying to come up with something to attract the attention of the unwary. Just treat that corner as being off limits.

Part 6 – Fire Bet

The **"Fire Bet"** has been around for awhile and is another means of separating the craps player's chips from the safety of the rail. Unless you are an accomplished dice influencer, you will see how fast your bankroll burns up.

The rules are simple. All you have to do is put a $1 to $5 bet in chips on the little designated circle in front of you located about eight inches in back of the Pass Line. The dealer will snatch your bet up and place it on a numbered circle corresponding to your location at the table. The bet is placed on your position number at the top of the proposition area in front of the box person.

The object of the game is for the shooter to make four, five or six different box numbers (4, 5, 6, 8, 9, and 10) as the point before the seven-out occurs. Repeating numbers don't count. Most casinos require you to have a Pass Line bet on board to play the Fire Bet.

Each time the shooter makes a point the dealer will place a fancy marker on the point made. To win, you have to make four different points or more before the seven ends the roll. If the shooter makes four different points the payout will be paid 25 for 1. Make five different points and the payout will be 250 for 1. If the shooter hit's the big casino with six different points, all the box numbers, the payout is 1,000 for 1.

Sounds simple! For a maximum bet of $5, this pie in the sky attraction could pay $5,000. How practical is the bet? Over the last couple years the **Fire Bet** has been with us, I have only hit it once for a four point payout. The 21 to 25% casino edge is not to my liking.

Part 7 – Hop Bets

A Hop Bet is where you call out two numbers that add up to the face value of a pair of dice thrown on the come roll or any other roll. It's a one roll bet.

You make the bet by tossing a chip to the proposition area on the layout and say, "Five, one on the hop," or "Sixes hopping five, one." If the combination five, one comes up, you win 15 times what you bet. If any other combination shows up, like 2, 4 or 3, 3 you lose.

Another way of betting on the Hop is to tell who ever will listen, the dealer. Stick or box person, that you want, "$3 all sevens hopping". This means you have all the combinations of the seven covered. (3-4, 2-5, and 1-6) If a seven is thrown you win $15. Press the bet and you will have $5 going on each of the three possible sevens for a total $15 bet. If the next roll is a seven you win $75. This can be an attractive bet for the accomplished dice influencer. How many times have you seen back to back sevens thrown on the come-out roll?

A $1 hop bet on the 1-1, 2-2, 3-3, 4-4, 5-5, and 6-6 outcome will get you $30.

Sounds simple but the percentages are too inflationary for my blood. This is a good bet for the whales who want to impress everyone how much they don't know about the game.

Chapter 26

Signature Numbers

There are several ways to determine your signature number or numbers. One of the best ways to find out what your signature number could be is to use "Bone Tracker", created by Mad-Dog. This tool will give you a lot of good stuff like if you are on axis, single or double pitching, what sets are best for you to come up with that signature number.

If my signature number was five, I would make sure I had a bet on it from the get go. It's very likely that six or eight will always be one of your signature numbers. If the point were 4, 9 or 10, I would place the 5 and 6. My odds on the point would equal the amount I had bet on the 5 and 6. That would be $25 on the 5, $30 on the 6 and 2Xodds on the point. $80 at risk! This can be scaled up or down based on one's buy in.

If 5 were my point, I would be inclined to put 4Xodds on the 5 which is allowed in Vegas. Then I would place bet the 6 and 8. My routine is to bet only three numbers until I have my initial bets off the board. My signature number would be the fist number I would consider pressing.

If you are really on your game, you might consider just betting your signature number if it is the point and loading up on behind the line with more odds. You can just place bet your number also and press right off the bat.

Keep in mind that your results on your practice at home may not match in casino play. If you are not throwing expected fours or tens, don't bet them. I think if you read the Part on how to work up to the Iron Cross play; you will see it is a way to work up to where you want to be with minimal risk.

If you don't want to bother with all the computer entries, there are other ways to determine your signature number. One such way which I call the "Signature Line Count" (SLC), is to count out 36 white chips. Use one set and one grip for all your tosses. Each time you toss the dice, place one chip on the number that you tossed etc. until your have used all 36 chips. You will see real quick what number stands out.

Take it one step further and throw another 36 tosses using red chips. Yes, it would be good to do another 36 with green chips. You will see right away what number or two numbers are starting to show up more than the others. If you don't have the chips or table layout you will have to stroke each toss on paper or make a chart.

I cannot stress enough on how your in casino results may and probably will differ from your home results.

Chapter 27

Sevens or Seven Avoidance

Using dice sets with the least amount of expected sevens is a major step in becoming a good dice influencer.

Setting for seven or setting for sevens avoidance is the heart of setting dice.

Your average player fumbles around with dice and then fires them down the table with no plan of execution. He or she more than likely will set a favorite number on top with no attention given to what numbers are on the sides of the dice.

A dice setter will set a specific number on top and then set a certain corresponding number on the side of the dice facing him... He or she will pick out a set from the basic six sets based on a certain axis. Three sets have only two expected sevens. The other three sets have four expected sevens. The object of the game is to avoid throwing sevens when shooting for the point.

The best way to do this is to use one of the sets with only two expected sevens. Too many aspiring dice setters get too taken up with chasing the point. They will stubbornly keep using the same set for a certain number until they seven-out. Once you zero in on a set that is resulting in everything but a seven, keep using it. Learn to play using the sets that result in less sevens showing up.

Remember that every time a number shows up that is not a seven; you get another toss with the dice. Look at that as a plus and concentrate on your next toss.

Dice setters just starting out have the tendency to use sets that they practice with. This is OK but they don't adjust their sets to real casino conditions. What works on the practice table may not work in casino play. You may find that your practice set keeps coming up point-seven.

There are several other factors that come into play under casino conditions! The hardness of the table is a common problem along with height of toss, speed and length of toss. This chapter is mainly concerned with the selection of sets to provide favorable results.

On the come-out roll we want to use the **"All Sevens"** set. If you establish a point right away, switch into your best sevens avoidance set and go to work. If your set is resulting in a lot of numbers, don't change a thing. Go with the flow till those sevens show up. Find a set that works for that particular session and stick with it.

Chapter 6 will give you an overview of the basic dice sets. Check it out.

Chapter 28

Handling a Nuisance

THE LOAD MOUTH

Every so often you will run into a jerk at the crap table that just won't keep his mouth shut or has his hands dangling over the rail.

He's got to say something stupid about every shooter and has no patience what so ever.

My last trip to Vegas, I had the displeasure of playing next to the most obnoxious, rude, loud mouth, S.O.B. that ever picked up a pair of dice. It was the closest I have ever come to going on tilt and telling the creep to take a flying leap on a pogo stick. This guy was a total nuisance with a capital "N". He fancied himself as a whale and was signing casino credit slips like there was no tomorrow.

I found out the hard way, why my preferred position was open at a full table. If the dice were not just a couple shooters away, I would have pulled an Irish and disappeared like the players before me, that didn't want to put up with his flack. It was the last night of my Vegas stay and I wanted some action, not a consternation with a sorry mess of human flesh that flunked "public manners 101", four or five times.

This guy was bum rapping every shooter on every toss. The table was ice cold. It was probably do to the negative vibes this jerk was spreading around the table. He was especially nasty to the dice setters. Everybody was setting the dice in some manner like they always do and he kept up venting his anger on each shooter as they seven-out. He kept saying, "Can't anyone shoot the dice around here?" He was directing all his remarks at me because the guy on the other side of him kept turning his back to him.

Against my better judgment, I decide to say something to him when he criticized a decent dice setter with a good toss. He said it loud enough for the shooter to hear. He said, "Hey, why don't you just throw the dice instead of fiddling around with them? You guys make me sick and waste more time and what good does it do you?" That's when I jumped in and said, "I'd be careful what I say if I were you, that guy had a one hour run last night." He come right back with, "I wasn't there last night and it didn't do me any good. If he's so good, why can't he do it now? I said, "you are absolutely right, why don't you try another table."

It was his turn to shoot and he quickly fired the dice about three feet over the stick guys head. They landed a foot short of the back wall, a pair of two's. I said, "Hey J- - -, (box person) that was a no roll, wasn't it?" The box tells the jerk to hit the back wall and I thought he was going to explode. Instead he says, yah, yah, I know. His next toss was another ridiculously high toss and came up short again but it was a seven and out. I said, "Gee you're no better than the rest of us."

I was in no mood to throw the dice, but it was my turn. I set for the C&E and bet $6 on it. It was a 5 and then I seven-out. The jerk says that figures. I said I won $24, how much did you win? He said, "Sh-t,#@$#."

I colored up and was leaving when the stick says, "Where you going, Charlie?" I said, "I'm going to get some fresh air. Somebody is stinking up this table."

HANDLING A RAIL BIRD

What about the guy that always has his hands hanging over the table down at the other end? Several players prior to my receiving the dice had their tosses deflected by this moron which resulted in seven-outs.

By the time I got the dice, things were getting pretty testy. My come-out toss just missed his hand and resulted in three, craps, and still no warning from the stick or box. My second toss just missed his hand again and was good for a point of six. I set for my next toss and noticed both his hands were hanging over the chip rail. Guys were yelling hands up, but this retard was in another world.

I said what the hell! Its time to waste a pitch! I threw a rising fast ball that hit him on the knuckles of his hand. He put his hand up to his mouth as if he was licking his wound. Everybody at the table started clapping. Hold on! That's not the end of it. After hitting his hand, up jumped a hard six. I said, "Would you mind putting your hands out there again so I can throw another hard six." We had no trouble with him after that.

Chapter 29

Tipping

Timely tipping by the Dice Setter can enhance his or her staying power at the tables.

Tipping is another key ingredient that belongs in the Dice Setters arsenal.

There are various ways of tipping the table crew. Members of the Dice Institute.com have indicated how they tip in the heat of the battle. In fact Dead-Cat, a Las Vegas local player of renown has just posted a reply on where to find his article on tipping.

The Mad Professor has some on going replies to the question and some of his past articles should be revisited. I especially like his suggestion that you tip only when you have the dice. This is the only logical way to tip. You want to be recognized for your tipping when it will do you the most good. Why tip when someone else is shooting? We want all the close calls to go our way when we miss that back wall.

Tipping after coloring up and preparing to leave the table, doesn't make much sense. If you haven't been tipping when you were the shooter, what good is it going to do you when leaving the table? You're gone. **Tipping** while you have the dice might have prevented some of those, "hit the back wall" comments.

I don't worry about tipping a percentage of my current roll. My tipping is automatically done on all come-out rolls.

This may seem like a lot, but it is not. You might throw a couple sevens and an eleven before establishing a point and then making the point. That means you have tipped $4 or $5 already, but keep in mind that you were winning money at the same time. If you throw a couple craps, you might want to hold back putting out that white chip till you establish a point.

I always make an additional odds bet for the crew when the point is four or ten. It cost me $2 for the pass line and odds bet for the crew to win $5 if I make the point. You will find that the crew will be encouraging you to make the point. I don't mind when the dealer announces that the crew is on the line. It serves two purposes. One, it wakes up the rest of the crew to the fact that someone is taking care of them. Second, it wakes up the rest of the players that there is some tipping going on and maybe they will take the hint to tip.

Tipping is a matter of choices. A few years ago I conducted a survey among the dealers, asking what type of tips they preferred. When I think about it now, the results were not surprising. The older dealers preferred a bird in hand rather than nine in the bush. This is to say they preferred a pass line or place bet. The younger dealers leaned toward the hard way bet and other proposition bets.

The "two way hard way" bets hardly get any kind of recognition. They are tossed on the table from all sides and the stick person has all she or he can do to get the bets placed, let alone announcing each bet.

Tipping Makes Life at the Tables Easy.

When it comes to tipping I realize that there are different strokes for different folks. What works for the locals in Vegas may not work so well on the Boats in the Midwest. Then there is the question how much is enough for a departing tip. Tossing a couple white chips on the table on departure can be embarrassing if you haven't been tipping throughout the session.

If your session lasted two hours at a full table and you only saw the dice four times going point seven out, that would have been a $4 tip on a night you lost a ton. Are you going to tip on departure for having such a rough night? If you feel you have to keep up your image, go ahead and toss them a green one.

If you are a conservative you might "piggyback" your tip on your pass line bet. Just put a chip on top of your pass line bet and announce that you have the crew piggyback on the line. That bet will stay there until you seven-out. It will pay even money to the crew during the come out cycle and every time you make a point.

Then again the Vegas locals have the luxury of picking and choosing their place of play and have dozens of options on where they want to do their tipping. We Midwest Boat players have only one option when we climb aboard a casino Boat. We must be doing something right because when we check in at the table the table crew, box and suit all greet us like family. Either they are welcoming us as suckers or glad to see some friendly faces.

You might find this conversation with one of the suits interesting. I had just colored up when one of the suits called me over and asked if I wanted our usual dinner comp. He then said can I ask you a question? I said go ahead, but that doesn't mean I will give you an answer. He laughed and said why do you always wait to play until you can play next to the stick's right? I said that's an easy one. It's the shortest distant to the back wall. It's easy to make my C&E bet. It's easy to talk with the box and stick. I don't need to be by the Don't Come box. Playing from the end of the table is too much hassle hitting the back wall. I'm right handed and can reach out and clear the stick easily. From the left side of the stick I have a tendency to backhand the stick in the nose.

The suit chuckled and said he never thought of it that way. I asked him if I could ask a question. He said, sure. I asked him why the casinos insist that both dice hit the back wall. He related that it was casino policy to assure a random roll. It was my turn to laugh. I said that's funny. All your dice setters strive to hit the back wall with both die to gain a favorable result. When one die doesn't make it to the back wall, you are assured of a random roll. Your policy maker needs a refresher course in modern craps. He said he agreed on that. I thank him for the comp and jumped ship.

Keep track of you're tipping and with a plan you will see you're tipping is a small price to pay for a night's entertainment at the crap table.

Chapter 30

Complementarities

Forget the Complementarities' (Comps)

Forget about all those *"Comps"!* The casinos have the crapshooter so worried about getting a comp that he can't see straight.

The pit critters make a big deal about marking their little cards right in front of you and then returning your players card with a "Good luck Charles" and then scurries over to the computer to make an entry and see what you have done in the past.

By all means use your player's card. That alone will usually get you a good room rate, called the "casino rate." Establishing a line of credit with the casino of your choice will usually help get you a couple "comp" nights. Beyond that, if you can't afford to pay for your room and meals, you don't belong in a casino.

Now if you are a high roller, the casino will roll out the red carpet for you. The high roller could probably buy a couple floors in the hotel, but he gets free rooms, food, and even airfare. Is it fair? The casinos think so! I realize they need their share of high rollers, but let's give the low roller a break once in awhile. Throw him a bone once in awhile and he will frequent that casino all the time.

Everybody is so paranoid about receiving "comp points." they throw caution to the wind. Their betting gets a little crazy. They bet more and more away from their normal pattern. This is what the casinos want. Don't fall into this trap. You should plan on paying for your food and room. Work your strategy at the tables and don't get caught up in the **"Comp Craze."** If you should get a *"comp,"* be thankful and count it as a profit. That said; let's get back to the point! Forget the *"comps"* and play your style of craps. Don't try to impress the pit bosses or anyone else. Just play your own method of craps and you will be at the tables for longer periods of play.

Who knows, maybe the floor manager will feel sorry for you and throw you a bone!

Chapter 31

Hookup Advice

We seem to be our own worst enemy when it comes to hooking up with other players.

We even go so far as to line up private tables at receptive casinos. This usually occurs at Crap-fests, seminars and big group parties. That's not exactly staying under the radar.

The casinos usually require a $500 buy in for a private table. They wouldn't do it, if they thought they would come out on the short end.

Then there is a group that openly touts their alleged long rolls on cable TV. There goes the neighborhood. It might be a good idea to review some sound advice handed down through the years by the dice guru's.

Any time you have a large group players trying to hook up, you will run into problems. We must be smart in how we approach the tables. Most dice influencers have two to four preferred positions at the table. In my case, I have four, SR1, 2 and SL1, 2. I have more confidence at SR. If these positions are not open, I will wait until they are, or I walk.

When arranging your hookups, try to keep the participating players down to three or four. Six or eight player trying to take over a table will still leave two or four players out of position. We need every advantage we can get and playing out of position isn't one of them.

Ganging up on a table that just opened is one way of getting all your buddies on the table, but it will be hazardous to your bankroll. You will have too many players out of position. Don't think that the pit critters are going to let six or eight dice setters stand around with out making some bets. The pit will catch on to your passing the dice around to the preferred shooters when you keep doing it. The hardest thing for a dice setter to do is pass the dice, when he is trained to wait for the dice.

When you take up a position at the table with your fellow DI's, don't call them by their "Handle." Refer to them as the "Shooter" or first name on their player's card. Don't talk shop at the table. Don't try to impress your fellow DI's with your betting. Same goes for the table crew and pit critters. They have seen it all. Play your regular style of game and qualify everybody at the table, no matter who they are. Good luck and may the dice Gods be at your table.

Chapter 32

Random Analogy

"Random Analogy" or how to play or not play a Random Roller...I thought it might be a good idea to take a look at the *Random Roller* with all the interest focused on them lately. Random Rollers take up most of the positions at the craps tables. They are called other names such as RR's, Randies, chicken-feeders and as of late, fleas.

What is a **Random Roller**? In craps lingo a Random Roller is someone expected to throw a seven every six tosses. The Random Roller's are shunned by the advantage players because of their ability to appear out of nowhere and clutter up the craps table with their nuisance bets and general lack of knowledge of the game.

There are several classes of **Random Rollers**. We have the common Random Roller that set the dice in some way so as to look like they know what they are doing and then just fire the dice down the table in any old fashion. Then there is the Random Roller that bets on everything. They have chips all over the board and are always questioning the payoffs. We also have the chip flipper who takes pride in seeing how far he can toss his chips into play. The last minute better falls into that class.

Where do they come from? They hide behind slot machines and cocktail waitresses. They are under the rug. I always look under the table before buying in. I wouldn't be surprised if they were walking around dressed up as Suits.

Betting on the **Random Roller** is real gambling at its finest. How's this new saying? "See a RR, bet a RR". Be my guest.

How to play them? The old school of thought advocates using the infamous "Five Count". Well, at lest you won't lose anything on the first five tosses. You might get lucky on that sixth toss when you put out that come bet. If it's a seven or eleven you win. If it is a box number, you go up in the box and are invited to put up odds that will put more money in jeopardy while the seven is now over due. Not for me. I would rather place the six or eight on the Random Roller from the get go and take my chances on his early throws rather than later on his over due seven expectancy tosses.

Random Rollers will get hot and when they do, you don't want to be setting on your hands while he throws number after number. If you have a number working and the Random Roller gets hot, he will make your number in the mix and you can expand from there.

Random Rollers can be your friends. They all fumble around setting the dice enough to keep the heat off you. If you suspect a Random Roller of being a dice influencer, check his toss first. If he has a consistent toss and landing the dice in the same area over and over, bet him. Don't worry about what he is setting. It's the results that count. Take note of what he is betting and follow suit.

Some of my best friends are **Random Rollers** who love the sport of craps but are too busy working or just too lazy to practice and learn what it takes to become a winner.

Chapter 33

Trip Reports

Good trip reports are the result of dedicated players wanting to inform the members of the Dice Community of events that accrued during their visit to various casinos.

I am interested in where they played and how they were treated by the crew and pit personal. Comps and table minimums do not play an important part in my casino considerations. The amount of money or units they won or lost is inconsequential. It's well enough to say I was satisfied with a win, or lost a bunch on the session.

What I find most interesting in a trip report, is the strange or unexpected things that happen during play. I enjoy hearing how the players and crew handle obnoxious kill joys at the table. In a previous report I related what happened when one of the Suits, during a chip fill, spilled six racks of chips all over the table and bets. It was wild. When they tried to clean up the chips they knocked over more stacks. Its things like this that makes entertaining reports.

It's good to know if you played on twelve or fourteen foot tables, but as far as hardness is concerned I would rather find that out for myself.

As far as heat is concerned, it is always good to know in advance if there is any forthcoming and should be in the report.

The characters you end up playing with could be the highlight of your report. Craps is just like golf. If you want to find out about someone's personality, just shoot a round of golf with him or watch him at the crap table. Sooner or later his true personality will surface.

Chapter 34

Superstitions

When it comes to believing in superstitions the craps players are right there at the top of the list. They are quick to jump on anyone or thing at the least provocation. Most of the time they are just making up excuses to cover up their short comings as a craps player!

Here's my favorite! When a player throws the dice and one die goes off the table invariably the shooter or someone else will yell, **"Same dice."** Why in the world would anyone want to throw dirty dice that have been on the dirty sticky floor? I always say give me some new ones. The dice influencer makes a point to have short finger nails and clean fingers so as not to stick on the dice. Those **same dice** guys are the first one to tell you "I told you so," when you seven-out.

Receiving sevens from the stick person is another one I like. If I am setting the all 7's set for the come-out, it saves me time setting and getting into my throw. The box-person will sometimes chastise the stick person for delivering sevens up. I just laugh! It's not going to affect my game either way. I am still going to have to throw the cubes down the table.

The **stick change** is another taboo. If you are in the middle of a good roll and they change the stick person, bad things will happen or you will seven out. Bah, humbug! Stick changes can be good. Especially when the stick is used for a fishing pole or the stick person has their oversize stomach hanging over the rail. Some players will turn their bets off for a throw or two when the dice leave the table or if there is a stick change during a good roll.

The Dice hitting someone's chips is another reason for the cry baby to have another excuse for his inability to perform and amaze us with his lack of skill. I love it when the shooter knocks over the dealer's stack of chips and the result is a hard six. Someone is bound to tell the shooter to keep hitting the dealer's chips that way. The dice influencer has a more practical reason for wanting to avoid the chips at the other end of the table.

Hitting someone's hand is another reason for our superstitious players to go bonkers when their results are less than stellar. Most stick persons will say, "Dice are out," as a warning to stop making bets. One stick person would add, "Hands up," just before the toss. Being from the Chicago area, I immediately started looking around for the guy with the gun.

Pre-toss antics such as rubbing your hand on the felt in a circular motion before picking up the dice! Throwing the dice up against the wall before picking out the number they want or shaking the dice next to their ear! Are these bad habits or are they just a superstitious routine they feel they have to do for a good result? First off, why rub the dirty felt with your shooting hand? Why waste time throwing the dice around before picking them up? They end up setting only a number on top and have accomplished nothing and top it off by listening to the dice being shook up by his ear. I wonder what they hear.

Chapter 35

Things That Go Bump In the Night

December, 2008

We have a lot of things to think about that some times cause us nightmares. They are the small bumps in the road that the casinos throw in our path to slow us down while they tell us to speed up play with only one or two players at the table. The "Grand Victim" casino boat in Elgin even goes one step further by posting a request that nobody should set the dice. This is one bump in the road that can be fixed by simply not playing there. There are better boats in the pond that are bigger, cleaner and intelligent people running them.

Saturday night at the boat brought out some of the every night nuisances we have to tend with. A randy was placing a late bet, down on the hook, at the other end of the table while Laser910 was having a nice run. Laser nails him on the knuckles and sevens out. Laser goes ballistic and wants to go and punch him out. It took a little while to calm him down. I told Laser if the guy puts his elbows on the rail again, I will nail him with a fast ball. Later on the guy has a nice roll and Laser goes over and tells him he made up for getting in the way of the dice.

We had been playing at a $10 table for a couple of hours and then they change it to $15. The next four shooters had to be reminded it was now a $15 game. Now it was my turn to goof up. I asked for a $6 C&E. Wrong! The stick says it has to be a $10 C&E at a $15 table. I said make it $12 and then threw two three's before establishing five for my point. I put $18 on the six and eight and want to balance it out with $10 PL odds. Wrong again! The stick says you have to put at least $15 odds on a $15 table. I put out $20 to get the proper payout.

Things were rolling right along and I had the Iron Cross set up and was into a good roll. The dealer, stick and box never missed reminding me to bet the C&E or renew my six and eight when I made one of them as the point. Two things they never did were to remind me to take my PL odds or replace my Field bet when I lost it to the 5, 6, or 8.

During the roll the stick slid the dice over to me with the seven on top. We both stood there looking at the dice. The stick got very apologetic and flipped them over to the point. I told him I wasn't superstitious; just give me the dice with the point on top. He did!

During play I asked why they didn't have the Fire bet on this table. The box person said that these two tables were reserved for high rollers and they didn't want it for them. Doesn't make sense to me! The whales usually go for the dumb bets.

Where did my favorite bet, the Big 6 and 8 go? Only idiots would make that bet. Now how am I going to be able to tell who the idiots at the table are? Now they have this over-under seven gimmick that I never see get any action.

Final bump in the night: Not being a proposition player outside of playing the game within a game, C&E bet on the come out only, I wonder what you have to bet on the other prop bets at a $15 table. How about the Hop bets?

Chapter 36

Saturday Night at the Boat Series

*The **Saturday Night at the Boat Series** is a collage of articles posted on the Dice Institute Forum from time to time. They tell of the experiences of four members of the Dice Institute known as the "Crew." Their ups and downs and observations along the way may help others in their attempt to become dice influencers.*

Saturday Night at the Boat I

December 3, 2006

It's been two months since I have been to the boat. They missed me so much that they sent me a $25 Cash coupon. So the Kooler and I landed at the tables at 8:15 p.m. I started sniffing around for some of that table energy at the only two tables that the once Trump Boat (now Majestic Star II) now provides. Both tables were $10. One was fully packed and so quiet you could hear a chip drop.

The second table was half full and no energy, but there was an opening at SL2 and SR2. The Kooler jumped in and I moved in at SR2. The guy at SR1 had the dice and seven-out fast, and left. I move over and noticed three don't players. Not a good sign. One of the don't players at SL1 had the dice and had a pile of green chips bet on the don't. I made my RR bet of placing the eight for $12, thinking this guy won't throw big red for awhile. He only threw one eight and some junk numbers, before the seven-out. The Kooler went point, seven and out. That was the only time he tossed the dice. He passed the dice the rest of the time we were at the table. He is skeptical of dice influencing, but he sure loads up when I have the dice.

One hour later, we were down $175 and decided to meet Target at the Resorts Boat (5 minutes away).

Resorts had four tables going and I still couldn't find any of that table energy some people are talking about. The Kooler took off for the poker room and I found my spot at a $10 table. I was trading chips on the RR's and losing more than winning when Target tapped me on the shoulder and said he would be at the $15 table across the way.

I decided to join him and ended up at SL1. Target (SR1) had the dice and was grooved in. I placed $30 on the six and eight just in time when Target hit an eight. He came right back with a six and another six. Five was the point and the next thing you know I had the iron cross up and working after placing the five for $25 and $15 on the Field. Target obliged by tossing box cars and several other Field numbers. It was a fifteen to twenty toss run that was profitable even though we left a lot of chips on the table.

It was my turn now and I opened with a good old eleven for a quick $42 in the rack. That's when JJR showed up with a pocket full of money from hitting a royal flush on the poker machines. I told him to jump in because I am beginning to smell some energy in the air. JJR bought in and made $175 on my roll. Then he had a nice roll himself. Next thing I know Target has the dice. Seems the guys at the other end of the table passed the dice all the way around to Target. The three of us had mini rolls and colored up. It was past JJR's bedtime, so he left.

While I was cashing in, Target had spotted his spot open at a $10, twelve foot table (Resorts has two twelve and two fourteen foot tables). I went over there and Target had the dice. He was hot and I threw $100 on the table and asked for a $30 six and eight. Target came through with two six's and an eight. Then it was over. Target says I'm $7 ahead, let's quit and get something to eat. I said after my throw. He said OK. When cashing out again, Target says, you're beautiful, I'm now $177 ahead. I just smiled and said lets find the Kooler and eat. The female suit gave us a comp for the meal.

Saturday night at the boat hasn't changed much. We had good table crews all night and the pit crews were friendly. Again Target and I were the only ones tipping the dealers. The only thing that bothered me was the fact that Target was setting the Hard-ways all night. But then you've got remember that he was trained by GTC.

The camaraderie we had at the tables was better than any untouchable energy or was that energy we created?

Saturday Night at the Boat II

December 10, 2006

Saturday night at the boat again! Well, I have got to pay for this site somehow. Laser wheeled us into the Resorts parking garage at 1930 hrs. I remarked to Laser, that we didn't have a full moon tonight and very few stars. There goes our astrology theory.

We spotted Target at the twelve foot table, we played on last week. There was three $10 and one $15 tables working. Target was at a $10 minimum table, SL1 and already down. I looked for the Gypsy occult person, but no luck. Laser moved in at SL2. Target had already talked to the tall fellow at SL1, if he would move over when I got there. He did and we all were in our best positions.

No excuses tonight. Well, maybe one. I had a terrible head cold and would have to throw clairvoyance and telepathy out the window I would have to rely on Muscle Memory. There was no energy in sight.

Looking over the table, there was ten of us. The three of us, two "Don't Pass" players, one dice setter with a good throw and four random players. The two "Don't" players always passed the dice. The random rollers were making points. We were never behind in chip count from the word go. When the young fellow next to me got the dice, the box guy says in fifteen minutes the table is going up to $15 minimum.

Bad move on the suits part. We all loaded up on more numbers while the table was still at $10. The young fellow held the dice for the entire fifteen minutes, making points and numbers. I told the fellow he was a hard act to follow.

As soon as I got the dice, they made it a $15 dollar table. Another bad move on their part!

It forced us to bet more and win more. We lost the "Don't" players and two or the random players. Now the dice will be coming around more often. I made a $6 C&E and $15 pass line bet and set for an eleven (six-six on top and five-five facing me). On the first roll I hit the eleven, pressed it up to twelve, threw a deuce, pressed again, threw a three, pressed, and threw another three.

Pressed again! On the sixth $6 press, $36, I threw another eleven (plus $252 on that last roll) on the seventh roll.

As soon as I got six for the point, Target and Laser were all over the hard six.

Game with in a game, the first phase was over. The second phase was just as good, making six the hard-way for Laser and making a couple other points. The guy next to me was copying my bets and was about $300 up. His girlfriend was bugging him to go so I said it would be prudent to color up right now and take your girl out to eat. He took my advice and color up with a nice profit.

Besides, how did I know Target was going to have an earth shaking roll? Target got grooved in for a nice run and energy was riding high. Anytime Target is at the table, there's going to be high five's and at-a-boys flying all over. For awhile everybody was having mini runs accept Laser. Laser was having one of those nights where he was throwing beautifully and getting nothing for his efforts. Yet, he won the most money of the three of us. He owes Target and me for all the hard-ways we threw.

The last time I had the dice, we had a controversial call by the box guy. I had just made a couple of points and was looking for a six. One die came off the wall and landed against Laser's odds bet. The stick says, "Call it". The Box guy jumped right in and called it seven. Laser yells for the instant replay camera. I yell for a second opinion. Everybody ended up laughing over it, even the Box guy.

All in all it was a good night, except for my head. I used the standard 3V, with the five-one toward me and the point of the V toward me. Two times I used the V2 chasing the four or ten and seven-out.

I am beginning to like the Resort's Boat more than the Majestic Star. Especially when they give you a thirty-six dollar comp for taking their money.

Saturday Night at the Boat III

December 24, 2006

We had a hell of a time parking at Resorts parking garage. Cars were flying by everywhere. I swear Laser was a stock car driver in another life. He landed the Lincoln so close to Lake Michigan you could hear the waves hitting shore.

Laser and I arrived at the tables at 5:50 PM and Target showed up two minute later. Our positions were open at a $10, 14 foot table, so we jump in. There was only one other player there, shooting from the "Don't" hook. As soon as we bought in, they started crawling out from under the rug and the table filled up.

I was just about to place a bet when The Clock (our new rookie) tapped me on the shoulder and ask if we had room for him. I said no problem and he sneaked in at SR2. We now had SR and SL 1 and 2 covered.

The Clock got the dice first and had a 16 toss roll to get us going. The only trouble was, he threw five nines and none of us were on it. Same thing happened when I got the dice. I tossed about fourteen times and never made a dollar.

The Target started throwing some numbers and we load up and went down in Flames. Laser had three tosses and out. This wasn't good. Laser took off for the video poker machines. Target says let's try the $15 table that they just opened up. Surprise, it was a $25 table. I said to Target, our spots are open on the $15, 12 foot table that was so good to us last week.

At this point we were all down about $250. We all had 12 to 14 roll hands and were about even. I made four passes and then got knock out by a stack of chips at the other end.

When Target got the dice, the fun and energy started. We were not getting any help from the tooth fairy but when Target threw that come out eleven with all of us on the $6 C&E a roar went up. We pressed up another $6 and I said, "Have you got one more in you?" Target gave me that look and came right back with another eleven. High fives all over and everybody were yelling one more time. Target obliged by throwing a third eleven.

One more press and the next throw was a hard six. That was $42; $84 and $126 in the rack and our losses were wiped away.

Laser came back in time to make a $400 come back and break even. Target was up $400 and I was up $451. The Clock was the big winner at over $600 due to all those nines he threw. That's his signature number and the rest of us refuse to believe.

Laser still has the softest toss of all of us, but right now he is snake bit. We have just been waiting for him to break out big time.

We were all using the S-6 or a permutation of it, for the come-out. I used the V-3 or a permutation of it (9-3), all night. We colored up and collected our $50 comp and headed out for steak and eggs. We played three and a half hours before we jumped ship. It was just another crazy Saturday night at the Boat.

Saturday Night at the Boat IV

December 31, 2006

Five men overboard at the Saturday Boat gathering! Man the buckets. Break out the life boats. The Clock, Target, Laser, Golfer and my self jumped ship with our pockets just about empty.

That fourteen foot, $10 cruiser got the best of us so we bailed out and swam to shore to regroup. We decided to board the twelve foot, $15 table. We took up positions on both sides of the stick guy. Five of us in a row and at our favorite table! We loaded up on Laser, but Laser's slump continued.

The Clock was next, but he was firing blanks. It was my turn and tossed nothing but junk numbers. Target took over and made a point. We were so excited that we jumped in with both feet and loaded up. We recouped about 30% of our losses when Big Red show up and knocked us off out perch.

Our anchor man, Golfer took over and threw so many sevens on the come-out I thought we wouldn't see a seven for days. Golfer's run was a good one but we were so busy trying to recoup our losses that we never got a count on his tosses.

We cut our losses by 60% and decided to hit the pit guy for a comp and go eat. Bad mistake! While we were feeding our over weight bodies, Golfer went crazy and put a fat 1,000 coins in the tray. With that roll, Golfer saved our Saturday night reputation.

After we ate, Target, Laser and Golfer decided to go back to the tables. The Clock and I decided we had enough swimming up stream for the night and jumped ship.

The rest of the crew can fill in the blanks on this report, while I lick my wounds and try to recover from this three week cold.

Saturday Night Disaster at Boat V

January 13, 2007

Saturday the 13th, a day in, infamy at the Boat. The four of us arrived at the Resorts boat at 6PM. Target had our four spots saved at our favorite $15 table.

They were just opening it up and we got a couple costly quick turns with the dice. Nothing was going right and when the smoke cleared the first hour, we were all down $500 or more. It was so bad we change positions to get the monkey off our backs.

Then Laser got the dice and threw three straight passes on the five and capped it by making the ten. The random roller next to him got hot and rolled for twenty-five minutes.

We were now down only around $100 and decided to take a break. The break lasted about as long as it took to walk from the $15 table to the $25 table. You guessed it. We gave back what we just recovered. Finally I said lets go eat. On the casino, of course!

After eating we went back to the $25 table for more punishment. The Clock got his clock cleaned. The Target's wallet was full of holes. Laser was banging his head against a poker machine and I was looking for the exit to get off the barge.

Looking back over the four hours, rowing up stream, I think we broke every crap rule there is. None of us set a stop-loss figure. We played way too many chicken feeders. We had no business playing at a $25 table with the way we were shooting. We played way too long. We had a chance to quit when almost even, but we went on tilt and came back for more. We did not pull down our bets when we had the chance.

Things were so bad that Target started using the five-count on the crew. I never found any set that would work, so I started to chase the point. No good!

The Clock and I agreed that we would not practice for a half hour or so before going to the boat. Ten or twelve tosses and were on our way from now on.

That's the way the Dice bounce. Just when you think you know what you are doing, you get knocked off your perch. Like the man said, the good, the bad, and the ugly and boy it was ugly.

Charles C. Westcott

Wednesday Night at the Boat

Feb 1, 2007

The Kooler and I climb aboard Resorts Boat at 8 pm sharp. Target was already in position and was fighting off a bunch of guys to save my position at the table. The Kooler immediately headed for the poker room. After settling in at the $15 table that contributed to last week's disaster, I noticed that there was twelve hungry players packed in at that twelve foot table. There wasn't anybody at the $25 table and as far as we were concerned it could stay that way.

The table was so choppy I thought the boat had drifted out to the middle of Lake Michigan. Meanwhile the guy next to me was getting some heat from the Box gal for not making any bets and asked him to back off the table. He argued back that he had been there all day and had lost $600 and was waiting to shoot the dice.

The Box girl got up tight about it and said he hadn't made a bet in over half an hour. He had four red chips in his hand and he kept arguing with the Box. Finally he stepped back just enough so nobody else could get in there.

The dice came around and this guy jumps back into his spot. The Box had the stick guy by pass him and set the dice in front of me.

Now I have to try and focus while this arguing is going on. I made a four and a six, but that was the end of it. I was more interested in the outcome of the Box vs. the lurker.

One of the pit critters came over and said bet or get. I think they had it in for this guy, because a lot of us were skipping a lot of shooters' and could have been called on it. A little while later, a couple of tall dudes were throwing the dice off the table on just about every other toss. One of the tosses went over a players head at the end of the table. Out of the clear blue sky, the Target says, "Hey! This isn't basketball! There's no backboard over there". That got everybody laughing.

None of this helped our game any, so we resorted to witch craft, ESP, voodoo and metaphysical organic vibrations to stimulate our

130

sixth sense. In other words, we were resorting to guessing when to play the Field.

Our system was simple. As soon as a five, six or eight showed twice, we would put $15 on the field. If it hit, we pulled $15 and left $15 up. If it hit again, we pulled it all down and waited for the 5, 6 and 8 to hit twice again. Over all, did it work? Nope!

We decided to jump ship and paddle over to the Majestic. The place was packed. The Kooler headed for the Poker tables and made a nice withdrawal. The Target was tired of fighting the crowd and decided to swim home. I decided to kill time while waiting for the Kooler by putting in a little play from SL-2 that just open.

The $10 table was now packed. Out of nowhere crawled this small guy with a big white cowboy hat. Of course he had to squeeze in next to me. He removed his hat and dumped a bunch of crumpled up $1, $5, $10 and $20 bills. I mean they were crumpled up into small balls or wads and just dumped in the center of the table covering up a lot of bets. It took the Box gal twelve minutes to unfold and straighten out the mess. The total buy-in came to $314, all in small bills. The five hours spent between the two boats hardly produced minimum wage. It was better than last week.

It could only happen **at the Boat.**

Saturday Morning at the Boat

Feb 5, 2008

That's right! Saturday morning at the Resorts Boat on Lake Michigan with the temperature 8 degrees! Target talked the crew into this adventure, so it's his fault that we spent eight hours looking like yo-yo's. Laser and I climbed aboard at 10:30 AM and found Golfer already flinging the dice. He already had four points to his credit and looked good.

Laser jumped in at SL2 next to Golfer and I went over and stood behind the stick guy. The box guy saw me and asked the big giant to move over.

By the time I bought in, Golfer went seven and out and a random roller at the end of the table picked up the dice and held them a half hour. It was a great way to start the morning out. At the end of his roll I was up $250 and Laser was up more than that.

The next shooter went down in two rolls and the next RR had a fifteen minute run.

Then the heavy dude held the dice for fifteen minutes.

One hour had gone by and I was just getting the dice. I made one point and down. It was all down hill from there. If it wasn't for the RR's we would have never lasted the eight hours.

We took a forty-five minute lunch break and went back for more punishment. We spent most of the day sniping at the six and eights.

At one point, I thought I had it going with the game within the game play. I was setting the straight sixes and came out with a seven, replaced my $6 C&E and threw two elevens in a row and came back with a twelve, pressing $6 each time.

Laser was going nuts. He caught the twelve with a lone $5 bet on it. I made a six and then tanked on the four.

Tall Bob and Target were at another table, also playing the yo-yo game. Nobody could get any sustained drives going. The dice gods must have been frozen out. I couldn't even get any psychotic inspirations.

At one point, Target took Tall Bob home and came back for more of the same. We played on three different tables, all $10 minimum.

I was going crazy trying to figure out what everybody was doing. Laser was bouncing back and forth, setting the V-3 and the hard-way. I don't know what Golfer was setting and Target was on the hard-way, V-2 and 3. I kept chasing the point. Nothing worked for very long.

When the smoke cleared and I got home, I found I had $57 more in my pocket than when I started. $7 an hour! That's not even minimum wage.

Saturday Night at the Boat IX

Feb 18, 2007

It could have been a lot worse. After taking a fifteen minute tour of the Resorts parking garage, we landed some where between the fourth and fifth floor. If I remember right, they only have four floors.

The place was packed. They had four tables going, two $10, fourteen footers of which were packed. The two $15, twelve footers that were almost full too.

Target was already settled in at SL-1 and had the dice. Laser910 jumped in at SL-2 and the Kooler headed for the poker room. I stood behind the stick which is a no-no but manages to get their attention. The box Suit saw me and I pointed my finger at the eight inch opening next to the stick. The box says, "All right guys move to the right and let the gentleman in.

The table was colder than skinny dipping in Lake Michigan with the temperature zero. Five point sevens in a row. That cleared out my end of the table. I tried the dark side. Now it was seven, point seven. Nothing was working including the cashier windows. Target says it's not working here; let's try the other $15 table. There were only seven of us at that table and two were playing the dark side and passing the dice.

The first two rounds were more of the same. It was so bad that I wanted to call Bush and have him declare the two tables a disaster area. Laser910 had that look on his face that said lets blow this popcorn stand. Target says after we shoot we're gone.

The guy next to me has the dice and is betting pass line, single odds and making only two come bets. He then proceeded to throw 9-9, 10-10, 4-4, 6-6. I was amazed at the back-to-back numbers he was throwing but couldn't bring myself to make a come bet.

When I got the dice, I was close to $600 down and so were the rest of the crew. The Dice Gods must have felt sorry for us because they let me go on a forty-five minute run, some forty tosses. Made a lot of numbers, but when I got four for the point, I couldn't make it. I refused to set for it because the V-3 was working and I wasn't going to change anything at this point. When the smoke cleared we were back to even.

We stayed and things got back to normal, point seven's for everybody. The last time I had the dice, I manage a fifteen minute mini-run. Earlier I couldn't make a four but on the last turn I rolled three fours in a row. It was just another crazy Saturday night at the Boat. We have got to get away from these Saturday nights at the Boat. It's like dope.

Going home I was $41 lighter than going, but think of the emotional ups and downs for an evening's entertainment.

Saturday Night in the Twilight zone

April 30, 2007

It was just another Saturday night boat ride in the twilight zone. We got to the tables at Resorts around 8 PM. The $10 table we picked out had two other players and both of our positions were open.

We were amazed that the tables were sparsely attended. The dice were coming around quickly but so were the seven-outs. For the first 45 minutes the four of us took turns making a pass or two and then quick seven-outs.

Finally Laser910 took over and started banging out points and numbers. Laser910 was the only one that could handle that table. The rest of us at the table never made more than two points during a roll. Between myself and the now four other RR's, it was a disaster. If it wasn't for Laser's consistency, the ATM machine would have been the big winner.

As it was, the night was ruined by an obnoxious jerk playing straight out at my side of the table. He kept calling us jerks for not passing the dice. We did manage to get the seven foot creep to move his bets off to the side when Laser had the dice.

Meanwhile Tall Bob was reported to have had a 32 toss run at the $15 table across from us. He left with Target with a tidy profit. Not to be out done, Laser topped that with his next roll that

got us all well. Laser had at least five rolls that were between 15 and 20 tosses plus the big one of 34. There was no doubt that Laser had brought his" A" game.

Two and a half hours of frustration on my part of the game and playing the RR's, even Laser's good rolling couldn't keep us out of the hole. I just couldn't adjust to the table conditions. Everything I tried failed.

The obnoxious jerk had gotten to me and usually I can put up with quite a lot. I told Laser, shoot and then let's scoot. A quick inventory showed us both down a little over a $100 for 2 ½ hour boat ride.

Thanks to Laser's shooting we survived another Saturday night at the boat with a minimal loss.

Saturday Night at the Boat Revisited

June 20, 2007

It had been six weeks since the crew has put in an appearance at the Boat and the rust showed. We climbed aboard the Resorts East Chicago Boat at 7:10 pm after circling the parking garage, looking for a place to land. We almost ran over the Target in the process.

The four tables were still there right where we left them. There were three $10 tables working and they were getting the fourth table ($15) ready to go. We hung around for ten minutes, noting that the cats at SR1 and SL1 at our favorite table were just about to jump ship do to the lack of chips in their rack.

SR1 open up first and SR2 and 3 were already open. Laser, Target and I moved in and set up office. Laser asked the dealer how weather conditions were and was told the table was ice cold. I said that's good, we didn't miss out on any big runs.

We bought in and noted that a whale had the dice and was tossing them high and they were coming down and sticking in the new felt top. The dice were new and sharp. There didn't seem to be any pattern to what he was setting, although I noticed he had the fives on top when he switched to the DP. He had a pile of black chips in his rack that didn't last long. Twice he bought $2,000 in chips while he was at the table.

The dealer said that he had just made two passes so we jumped in. The whale obliged by making two more passes before the big red showed.

The Clock showed up and joined us on the hook. SL1 and 2 opened up and Laser and Target move over to their spots. Now there were ten at the table with two cats passing the dice. That left four of us and four random rollers. The first go around found each of us making a point or two and out.

We just had too much on the table when the seven came. The random rollers were no help at all. The whale was now staying on the dark side with huge DP bets.

The Clock was struggling but kept putting chips on the C&E and losing. Nobody hit an eleven all night. We quit the game with in the game. We were all down $100 to $200 when it happened. Laser had the dice and threw a come-out seven. He came right back and threw another seven. I asked the Stick-guy if they had the hopping sevens bet. He said no, why? I said my friend is in his seven mode. The Laser threw his third seven and I said to the box, are you sure you don't have the hopping sevens bet? He smiled and shook his head no. Laser tossed again and up jumped the seven again. Now the whole table is getting excited except for the whale playing the "don't pass".

When Laser tossed his fifth seven in a row, I had a tear in my eye thinking of all the money lost on not being able to play the hopping sevens bet. I asked the Stick how much would it have paid. He said he couldn't figure it out. Maybe some of you math guys can figure it out, playing a couple different ways Laser went on to have the roll of the night. Target said it was Saturday night and we were in no mood to go home. Looking back at the evening (2 ½ hours) it was the same old pattern, betting on the random rollers and betting too much on each other. We would just get loaded up on board and big red would knock us of our perch. Still it was only a $92 loss and a complementary pizza. Target said it was great to get the crew out of moth balls and get back into action. Laser put it best when he said you can't beat the camaraderie and excitement of the game. The Clock, still recovering from all those C&E bets, said at our age it's almost better than sex.

Saturday Night at the Boat, Man Overboard

June17, 2007

Laser and I arrived at the Resorts boat on Lake Michigan around 7:30 pm. There was plenty of parking spaces available but no sign of The Target. We thought it might not be so crowded this trip. Wrong! The place was packed and so were the crap tables. We stood around the tables for twenty minutes waiting for our positions to open up. Nothing was happening. Where was Target when we needed him? He's always the first one there and manages to save us spots. He must have fallen overboard or he would have been at the tables. We were not about to drag Lake Michigan for him.

Finally a spot at SL2 opened up and Laser jumped in. Ten minutes later, Laser was about to get the dice when the hook by Laser opened up and I moved in just in time for his roll. We were on a fourteen foot table and things were not going well at all. After we each threw the dice twice, we decided to quit and write the night off.

On the way to the cashier cage we stopped at the twelve foot, $15 table to watch the action. Laser was at one end and I was at the other end, observing the action when we both notice a shooter that had GTC training written all over him. He was at SL1 and had a beautiful toss and was setting the V3. Laser and I jumped aboard his roll and collect a few chips. After the big red showed up, Laser got to talking to him and low and behold he was none other than Clubsodakenny, a member of the Dice Institute.

We decide to hang it up for the night and comp out at Miller's Pizza and had a nice discussion with Clubsodakenny. I think we might have found a new member for the crew. We jumped ship about 9:45 pm and still no Target. I guess we will just have to put him on the DL until we can arrange to have the lake dragged.

Saturday Night at the Boat Explosion

June 2007

Saturday night at the Resort's Boat exploded with DI intensity. The Kooler and I climbed aboard at 7:10 pm after circling for a landing on the forth floor where we found a parking spot with a view of the lake.

The Kooler immediately headed for the poker room. I headed for the restroom much to my sorrow, because Clubsodakenny was at SR-1 and exploding the dice off the back wall making points and numbers. I should never have stopped to wash my hands because it must have cost me hundreds of dollars.

Clubsodakenny was hot and he had the dice smoking. I managed to get in on the tail end of his run and caught a few numbers before big red showed up.

The Target was at SL-2 and promised the guy at SL-1 a hooker or something because the guy switched places with him. Target then exploded with a number run. He was approaching close to twenty rolls when one die hit some chips and put his fire out.

Target must have said something to the brothers at the end of the table because they all passed the dice. A young stud by the dealer corner proved that a RR can be explosive too. He had a decent run, but his two pals flamed out point seven. The young lady with them had a nice turn shooting from the hook and spraying the dice all over the place but throwing numbers. It was at this point that the dealers were bringing green into play and exchanging them for red. They were down to the last row of red and needed a chip fill fast. You could see the dust circles.

It was my turn and I said that was some tough acts to follow. Clubsodakenny said lets make some money. Target already had the pass line cleared out of bets. I exploded out of the gate with back to back six's. Target scolded me for taking so long to make the point. I made points of eight, five and was working on the nine when the chip fill came. The dealer said, "Don't stop, Charlie, we got plenty of red now". More numbers and I had the Iron Cross set up.

Things were going along good till the right die took off and crashed into the dealer's stack. The seven put my flame out and it was Clubsodakenny's turn. I requested a come-out eleven and Clubsoda said okay and threw an eleven. It was that kind of night. Then Clubsoda and Target went point seven-out. Target said let's jump ship and head for the bank. We agreed and Clubsoda and I went up to the forth floor and dragged the Kooler out of the poker room before he lost his XXXXL shirt.

In retrospect, I only shot the dice once and the other's shot only twice. We played an hour and a half. We were on our favorite $10 table and had our favorite crew and pit critters. It was a night the DI's exploded for a short hit and "get" and all showed $300 plus for a short nights work at the office.

Sorry I almost missed reporting the funniest event of the evening. I was kind of busy at the time and I was over at SR-2 and couldn't see past Clubsoda. I heard the guy yelling come on CW, throw that nine. Then there was that chip fill going on while napkin ear Target was keeping the mine field clear of pass line chips. There was chips flying all over the place and when I threw a hard six or eight the table went nuts. My tunnel vision was working nicely but maybe I should have borrowed Target's napkin. The way the Random rollers were throwing the guys down at the end of the table needed flack jackets, hard hats and now ear plugs. Oh well, it was just another crazy Saturday night at the boat!

Saturday Night at the Boat

July 1, 2007

Saturday night at the boat was a show of different skills in shooting and setting. We arrived at 6:30 pm, a little earlier than usual, and found our positions open. I will leave Clubsodakenny tell you about the meat of the session. He did a fabulous job of counting our tosses and I kept track of the time with the dice. Lazer910 was busy entertaining a couple of friends from the golf course who managed to find us and were waiting for the magic to start.

On Laser's advice they bought in just as I got the dice. Laser has a habit of putting pressure on me. If he isn't piling chips on the hard six, he's yelling at me for taking so long to make a point. If that wasn't enough, he now has his friends loading up, just like it was show time. On the way home Laser said they made $450 on my roll and then put it all into a slot machine. Some people need a classic course on money management 101. Laser asked "them" how much they were up and then told them to jump ship with the dough. Getting back to the showcase of shooting styles, we had the dude who looked like he just got done milking the cows. He was shooting from straight out, setting the dice and stacking them before the toss which was aimed at the corner. I think his best was nine on the count meter. In the dealer left corner was a parade of transit shooters who never lasted beyond their point seven. The dealer right corner was occupied with another point seven specialist.

Shooting from SR-straight out was a tall seven foot dude who was a flinger but the life of the party. His wife was leaning up against a post behind me and he asked if she was bothering me. I said no, she's got my back. She was over six feet herself.

The tall dude kept saying the other end of the table better start helping out. He was trying to get them to pass the dice to us. Clubsodakenny was setting the 3-V (SR2) and slipping into my position at SR1 to make his toss. It was great. When I would step back for Clubsoda's toss, the stick-guy would also move back.

It's great what a little tipping will do. In spite of Clubsoda's GTC training, he is going to make his mark in the dice community.

Laser locked in on the 3V set and stuck with it. He came up short quite a few times and nobody said a word. There was no way this table crew was going to cut off their nose to spite their face. Laser hit it big time on the hard six. As far as my throw was concerned, my fingers felt good and I had my toss locked in the way I wanted in spite of the mine field the farmer had out there. I used the 009 set all evening. I think I will have it patented.

The crew is trying to decide if they should go to the boat next Saturday night. After all it will be the seventh day of the week, the seventh day of the month, and the seventh day of the year of 2007, buy in at 7 pm and at seven minutes after seven bet the sevens hopping and throw a seven.

Saturday Night at the Boat...7-7-2007= Zero

July 7, 2007

Laser and I arrived at the Resorts Boat at 6:25 pm and found Tall Bob at SL1, Target at SL2 and Clubsodakenny at SR1 at our favorite table. All four tables were working. The two fourteen foot tables were $10 and the two twelve foot tables were $15 and $25. Our table was $15 minimum.

Laser moved in at SL3, a bit out of his range. Clubsodakenny moved over to SR2 and let me in at SR1. A little later the Clock showed up and ended up playing straight out.

The first time around the table nobody had more then six or seven tosses. Tall Bob threw a couple sevens and an eleven on the come out that help the kitty a little.

The second go around was a little better. The random rollers at the table all passed the dice to us for most of the time we were at the table. They were familiar faces from out of the past. We picked up the pace a little with Clubsoda giving us a couple of numbers and a point in seven or eight tosses. I got it going for seventeen tosses with a couple of passes and some numbers.

Tall Bob was next and ran up a sixteen toss hand including some come out sevens and an eleven. Target got us all loaded up with seven or eight tosses before his enemy the "Big Red" knocked us out. Same thing happened to Laser. A "randy" went point seven and the Clock passed the dice, along with three other random rollers.

The next round deteriorated even more. I managed twelve tosses and got us all pretty loaded up when the seven knocked me off my perch. From that point on it was six tosses and out for everybody.

Target bailed out first, saying we just don't have it tonight. Clock never did get to throw the dice. Tall Bob followed Target to the exit. Laser says "Get us a comp and let's go eat". Clubsoda said he wanted to throw one more time. When I came back from cashing out, Clubsoda still was throwing. I asked Laser how long he had the dice. Laser said, "since you went to cash in." I threw $100 on the table for chips and Clubsoda sevens out.

That's the way the night was going. We ate and jumped ship and paddled home. After taking inventory and considering the cash coupons I cashed in, I discovered I was only down $120.

When I reflect back on the evening and see what could have been what should have been and what would have been if we would have used some of the knowledge available in this book. It was a good lesson to take to the "Great American Crapsfest" coming up. When you have six shooters and friends at the same table, protect your money and make them all qualify. Forget their past performance and judge them by what you see now. They are only as good as their last throw and that was a seven-out.

When you have a trend in a session where each shooter is getting in six or seven tosses, we should of taken a "hit and get" on each shooter. Greed was our down fall, thinking that each shooter was going to roll forever.

GAC attendee's take notice! Go slow. Don't be so quick to jump on the play of the named players or your buddies. Make them earn the right to have you bet on them. That goes for your self also. We all will have bad sessions. In this game it is two steps forward and one step back or is it one step forward and two steps back.

Saturday Night at the Boat Let Down

August 5, 2007

After five days in Vegas, Saturday night at the Resorts Boat seem to be a big letdown. Laser910 and I arrived at 6:30 pm and in ten minutes had our positions at SL and SR1 at our favorite $10 twelve foot table. The dice were jumping all over the place. The table layout looked the same but conditions felt strange. I don't remember the table ever being this bouncy. Several of the RR's were playing the Don't Pass and passing the dice.

By the time I bought in, Laser had the dice and already had thrown a come-out seven. I decided to wait until he established a point. Bad move. He threw another seven. I waited again and he throws nine for his point. I place the six and eight and Laser makes the point. I jump on the pass line and Laser gets ten for the point. I add the five and nine to my place bets and Laser sevens-out. Boy! Am I out of sync! For my take on being in sync with the game, game at hand, everything you try backfires. Laser had two decent rolls of twenty minutes and both times that I got to the point where I had the Iron Cross set up, he seven-out.

Laser and I both threw a lot of sevens on the come out to the point where we ignored the C&E bet. One of the RR's went on a six binge and threw six six's in eight tosses. It came at a time when all I had out there was a placed Six. I didn't press, I just collected. Laser got to shoot four times and I had three turns with the dice. After Vegas, it was a big come down and I missed the option to move to another table or casino. The table crew was only 50/50 as far as being efficient with pay outs and how they handled the stick. The box and suits were super polite. The bottom line was on the plus side when you consider the $30 cash coupons. Laser was up $29 and thanks to the Randy and his Six's and Laser's last hand, I was up $116.

Saturday Night at the Boat Traffic Jam

August 26, 2007

There are three ways to go to our favorite Boat on Lake Michigan. They all take about 35 minutes travel time. One route was under water from the storms we been having. The second route was under road construction. We took the third route and run into the detoured traffic from route one. What a mess!

The route we took along Lake Calumet, the water was so high that Laser said we should have brought our fishing poles. I said, yeah and we could troll for carp, right out the car window.

We finally reached our destination an hour later at the Resorts Boat. We walked up to our favorite table and within seconds we were in our preferred positions at SR1 and SL1. It didn't appear very crowded. One of the dealers said they were being hurt by the new Four Winds casino in Michigan which is only forty minutes away.

While we were buying in, a Randy had just made his point and was about to come out. I put out a token pass line bet and when he threw a five I took single odds and was ready to sit out the rest of his roll. He came right back with a five and I had a payday already. I put out another PL and he got ten for the point after throwing a couple come out sevens. He made the ten and on his next point we threw the six and eight into the mix.

Timing and getting into the flow of the game early eases the strain on your bankroll. The Randy gave us a cushion to work with and at no time were we behind or trying to catch up. After Laser and I each threw the dice once, we were up over $250. Laser suggested we leave but decided to stay after fighting all that traffic to get here.

The table wasn't crowded and the dice were coming around quickly with a couple players passing the dice.

The first three times with the dice I threw three elevens on the first come out roll. I told Laser I was just tuning up for the Hilton tournament.

We played two hours and for the most part everybody throwing the dice made some points and held the cubes for at lest five minutes. It became a hit and run game. There was very few point sevens. I was pressing on the first hit and taking home on the next hit.

The one Randy I didn't play, ended up throwing five six's in a row. The next time he got the dice, I put $30 on the six. Two throws later he threw a six. I brought it all home and he seven out on the next toss. When you're in sync with the game, life is good.

Here are a couple of after thoughts. Once again we had an excellent table crew. Everybody was on a first name bases and the pit critter was friendly. They still do not allow "hopping sevens". The table seemed less bouncy than my last visit but then I felt I had better control this trip. I used a variety of dice sets chasing the point. The standard V3 seem to have the best longevity.

How did we do? Laser made enough to fill up the gas tank and I made enough to buy into a $100 poker game.

On the way home we managed to avoid the high tide, flood area, road repairs and traffic jam and made it back to civilization in 35 minutes.

Saturday Night Musical Chairs

September 2, 2007

The crew climbed aboard the boat at 6:40 P.M. There were four tables working, $5, $10, $15 and $25. Naturally the $5 table was loaded. The $25 table empty. The other two tables were sparsely populated.

I spotted Golfer at the $10 table at SL1. SR1 was open so I jumped in, even though it was the fourteen foot table I didn't like. The Kooler headed for the poker room and Golfer and I took it on the chin for about an hour with no luck or skill. I even joined him on the dark side but the sevens on the come out and the point sevens right after- words sunk us deeper.

We moved over to the $15 table which is my favorite 12 footer. Things were so bad at the first table even the crew suggested we move to another table. After the move I found myself at SL2 which added to my problems, being I am SR oriented. This table was so bad they lowered the minimum from $15 to $10.Golfer and I decided to take a pizza break.

The Klock showed up and found us eating pizza. Golfer suggested we go back and give it another try. Reinforced by The klock, we found ourselves back at the first table. The Klock had a nice ten minute run which was the highlight of the evening. The Target showed up after escaping from the Horseshoe. He ended up on the good table by himself. In that last go around of musical chairs we

were playing, an interesting thing happened. I had an $18 Six and eight and a $10 five on board. The random roller seven-out. I turned to say something to the Klock and when I turned back the next Randy was coming out. My bets were still up at our end of the table and the other end was void of all bets.

The dealer had a funny look on her face, the box guy was watching the other end of the table and I was trying figure out what happened or if I missed something. It didn't matter much because the Randy went point seven and out. The dealer was new and needed help on a couple of occasions. It was a lesson learned for the evening! If you don't practice and insist on playing random rollers on the wrong tables out of position and you're out of sync, it's time to regroup.

Saturday Night at the Boat Reserved

Sept 16, 2007

Saturday Night at the Boat started out great when Laser and I found a parking spot so close to the entrance that I thought we were in the handicap parking area. Then when we got to the Crap area we saw that our favorite table and crew were roped off and had reserve signs all over it. I jokingly said to Laser, "Look they are expecting us."

At this point Clubsodakenny joined us and said the table was reserved for some high rollers. The table was marked $10 minimum and no one in sight. I went over and asked the suit what was going on and he replied that they were holding the table for some guest. I said, were here and he laughed and walked away.

The other two tables where loaded with Randies, so we went back over to the reserved table and found two players in action. One of them was big John who we had played with on previous Saturday nights. I said, maybe he will let us join them. Two weeks ago I had a big run that filled up his chip rack. Clubsodakenny said that big John was a guest of the high roller who looked like he should have been on trial for something.

Ten minutes later they were gone. We asked the suit what is going on and are you going to open up the table to us low rollers. He said maybe in twenty minutes if none of the special guest return. We also noticed that there were four or five other suits with walkie-talkies plus security guards hanging around. Very strange!

After this discussion with the suit we were joking around with the stick gal and told her to put the reserve signs on each side of the stick while we waited things out. She did with Clubsoda's help.

Finally we got on the table in our reserved positions and went to work. It was another one of those choppy nights were you had to take a hit and run for cover. I set a new record for myself by pulling down my bets four times.

Laser started out OK but things turned sour and I even caught him using the hard-way set. Clubsoda gave us an eleven and some

Charles C. Westcott

craps numbers on the come-out. Our come-out game was the only thing working for awhile.

I think the third time I got the dice, I got a break. I came out with my second eleven and followed with a twelve and a three. Then I made back to back six's for the point and Clubsoda got on my back for taking so long. My next point was four. I set the standard V-2 and went on a six, eight binge. So be it. I didn't care what number was coming up as long as it wasn't the dreaded red.

I noticed big John was back at the table and had three or four black chips on every number and twice as much on the four and ten. Everybody was yelling for the four and big John says, forget the four, keep throwing numbers. Finally I made the four and the table went nuts. We were all just about even now and then everything went down hill.

Laser headed for the slots and Clubsoda and I hung around for another point seven and out. It was time to pack it in and hit the suit for a pizza comp. The suit said you had it going there for awhile. I thanked him for reserving the table for us and he just laughed.

Saturday Night at the Boat, Clinic

October 7, 2007

The evening started out simple enough. Laser calls at 5:15 pm and says, "lets go test the water, I'll pick you up in a half hour". I said fine, that will give me time to warm up with a few practice throws. I set the 009 permutation of the V-3 and threw twenty times before I threw a seven. That was it! No more wasting any runs before we get to the boat.

We arrived at the boat at 6:45 pm and found all four tables had only two or three players. They were all $10 tables. Laser and I settled in at our favorite table at SL-1 and SR-1. There were two random rollers at each end of the table. Two of them kept passing the dice. We had played with them before.

We waited out one randy and I got the dice. It was a good start that lasted for about ten minutes. In fact the next three turns with the dice, lasted ten minutes or more. In the mean time Laser was struggling. He caught that disease called "point seven and out". I felt sorry for him. We all have been there and know the feeling of helplessness.

I was the only one at the table that seemed to be immune to it. I kept us above water until that final roll that lasted over a half hour. Laser remarked that it was too bad they didn't have the Fire bet. He said I made five of the six box numbers during that roll. During one of the come out tosses, Laser put $5 on the twelve and on the next shot I threw the twelve. I thought Laser was going to kiss me, but he restrained himself.

During the session I gave Laser two elevens, a twelve and a hard eight and four C&E craps and a bunch of sevens. Does it pay to tip? During the come-outs I was betting a $6 C&E, and a $10 PL with $1 along side for the dealers. I threw a seven and the stick guy removed the C&E bet. When this happens I normally don't replace the C&E and set for the seven until I get a point. On the next throw after the seven I threw an eleven. I remarked to the stick, "I guess I blew that one."

At this point the dealer said "throw down $6". Then the stick says, "Pay $42."

I put another white chip on top of the one already out there. I got four for the point and put two more white chips for odds on the dealer bet. What really made it good was that I eventually made the four. I don't know if anybody else caught it, but Laser did. Both the dealers and I showed our appreciation and everything was cool. I thought Laser was going to get it going, the last time he had the dice, but as soon as we got loaded up on board, he went down in flames. I was getting tired and hungry and suggested we color up and get something to eat. While coloring up, I pointed to my mouth to the friendly Suit for a comp. On receipt of the comp he asked what I bought in for. I said $400. He said, "Well you sure put on a shooting clinic tonight". I know someone will want to know what the bottom line was. It was $300 plus. For the most part I chased the point and used the 009 set a lot. I wasn't happy with the way the dice were coming off the back wall, but," if it isn't broke, don't fix it".

Saturday Night at the Boat, Wounded!

October 14, 2007

Saturday Night at the Boat with the walking wounded. We should have gone to the hospital instead of the boat. Prior to leaving for the boat, Laser's heart monitor zaps him in the shower. He says it was like being kicked in the chest by a mule and he saw blue. His wife suggested he stay home and Laser says, "Hey, this is Saturday night."

One hour later, Laser comes by my place and says lets go. You drive in case I deep six. By the time we got to the boat, Clubsodakenny was already there re-coning the tables. Our favorite table was just opening up at $10 minimum. We got our positions and the stick handed me the dice. It turned out to be a low count toss night. Eight or ten tosses and out. We just didn't seem to be in the right mental mood.

Friday night we practiced at Clubsodakenny's place and I thought we were ready to play. It was give and take for about an hour until Clubsodakenny got the dice and went on a 34 toss hand. He brought us back. Clubsoda was just coming off the disabled list with a bad case of stripe throat, but it didn't affect his game.

I wasn't in top form either, due to back problems but we gave it our best shot. Right after Clubsoda's big hand of 34, they change the table to $15 minimum. Clubsoda says let's go home and lick our wounds. I was worried about Laser and agreed.

Laser and Clubsoda were down a little bit and I was up $50. We were glad to escape at this point before we went down with the ship.

Saturday Night at the Boat - Home Coming

November 18, 2007

After five days playing in the desert, it was good to get back on the water. When we found a parking spot close to the casino door, I told Laser that's a good sign it's going to be a good night.

Clubsodakenny is going to give a more detailed report. I just want to touch on the weird stuff that happened. Laser and I met Clubsodakenny standing around the four loaded tables of players. The tables were really loaded, but Clubsoda and Laser squeezed into their regular spots. The SR side of our favorite table was packed, so I stood around watching the action for about twenty minutes. Finally I jumped in on at dealer left hook.

A couple of the brothers left, so I slid over to SL3 next to Laser. I no sooner put a bet down and the guy at SR1 seven- out and left. That's when the stick guy says, "Hey Charlie, you want your spot?" I said sure and moved again. The stick then says, "Do you want to shoot the dice?" I'm thinking this is great; all of a sudden I get the dice. The box guy was about to say something when the stick says it was OK because they are all buddies.

Before I could even get my bet moved over to SR, the crew had $6 C&E's on board. I did likewise and the brothers jumped on the horn. It was a good opening salvo. I threw three 3's, a 2, two sevens and then got six for my point. I made the six and seven-out.

Clubsoda then went to work and the six and eights were flying all over the place. He even threw an eleven on the come out. Laser then took over and went on a hard-way kick. The crew was in the building.....er, boat.

One of the brothers didn't want us to have all the fun and went on a forty-six minute run. Laser was jumping all over the hard-ways while Clubsoda and I were pressing the six and eight while the iron was hot.

It was right in the middle of all this action that the brother had nine for a point and let loose with a throw that sent one die bouncing of a girl's chest. The dealer called no-roll at that point but the die bounced off her and came back on the table. The box over ruled the call and said good roll, point nine made, pay the line. I said, "Let's watch those quick whistles."

The hot shooter had another close call when the same dealer called seven on a cocked dice up against some chips. The box guy jumped in again and said it was a six.

The shooter never once made a bet for the table crew, but we were betting on the line on every come-out the guy rolled. It paid off.

After he seven-out, I told Clubsoda that there will be three or four quick seven-outs now, so go easy. Sure enough the next two shooters went point seven and so did I. Clubsoda threw a couple of numbers and he was out. Laser broke the ice and had a decent run. Him and those hard-ways, they just kept coming.

We were in the process of coloring up when I noticed everybody had left the table. I said I'm going to shoot. I had a bad taste in my mouth after that last seven out. All three of us had fair hands and quit on a positive note.

Saturday Night at the Boat Full Moon

November 25, 2007

On the way to the boat I remarked that there was a full moon. I said I usually shoot good with a full moon, but watch out for the weirdoes that come out.

Upon arrival we found Clubsodakenny at SL1 and Target at SR1. Laser slipped into SL2. I went over by Target and kidding ask him what he was doing in my position and that he belonged on the other side of the stick. Target said no problem and asked the guy on his right to move to the hook. Target moves to SR2 and slips me into SR1. Most of the guys at the table were there last Saturday night, including "Big John" who had the dice and just made a point.

You don't want to mess around when "Big John" has the dice. He is a black chip player that does not set the dice and always shoots from the dealer hook. "Big John" releases the dice and one of the cubes takes a high bounce and almost lands in the cleavage of a low cut blouse at the other end of the table. We complimented him on his accuracy. I asked Target what the odds were that he put one down that V access between those two side bumpers. "Big John" had a nice hand that got us loaded up on board when big red showed up.

Target was our lead off man but he couldn't get on base. I was next and had a fair fifteen minute hand that got three points and some numbers. Clubsoda had a 16-18 toss hand with a bunch of come-out sevens. Laser went on a six, eight binge for about fifteen minutes and was on the hard-way kick. The first round wasn't too bad; three out of four of us having fifteen minute rolls and had some help from "Big John."

That first round was the best of the night, but after that we couldn't do anything. We gave it all back and then some. We were at our favorite table but they were breaking in a new dealer and it slowed things to a crawl. Target was out of position and his arrows were missing the target. We had a lot of other players passing the dice to us, but we all got into four rolls and out mode.

Target was the first to check out and we weren't far behind. We can't blame it on the full moon, or can we?

Saturday Night at the Boat Slaughterhouse

December 23, 2007

Well, it had been three weeks since we had been to the Boat on Saturday night. We had good intentions of going West to Joliet but Clubsodakenny suggested that we g to Indiana where we know we can get our spots at the table on Saturday night.

Thirty-five minutes later we were touring the parking garage for a place to land. We finally found a parking spot with a view over Lake Michigan. I suggested we call a cab to get to the casino.

The two of us finally reached the tables and found three working with six players at each table. The good table crew was split up and our favorite table had all new faces except one. We opted for the twelve foot table and settled in at SL1 and 2. It was then that I noticed that the jerk from the last time we were here had the dice. Two tosses and out he went. Next thing I know Clubsoda had the dice after a number of players passed. I guess they didn't want the wrath of this guy's heckling while they were shooting.

Clubsoda made a couple points and I though we had something going. No such luck! I went down in flames too. The clown mumbled something about passing the dice. At this point SR1 opened up and I moved over to it fast. So did the guy on my left. I told the stick we had to get away from the jerk. The stick said, "Hit him with dice they are new and sharp".

It was Christmas and I thought better of the idea. I did however use my intimidation toss. The jerk was playing from straight out and I held the dice shoulder high and point them straight at him and held the pose and looked him in the eye. If he would have said something, I might have flicked the dice right at his chest.

Mr. Jerk had his bet right in my landing zone so I started aiming right at his chips. Three times in a row I hit his chips and even made a point. The next time I hit his chips I seven out. I remarked that his chips caused the seven.

I will say this! He was the only one at the table to make three points. When he got the dice, everybody bet the "don't pass line at my end of the table. Wouldn't you know it? He went on a three point binge, and said, "Are you guys down there believers yet?" The dealer at our end said, "Pass the dice", when he made his points. The dealers were even fed up with him.

It was a typical Saturday night at the boat with something weird happening. Where was Laser910 when we needed him? We lost our shirts and it was a long cold walk to the car.

Saturday Morning at the Ice Boat

Jan 4, 2008

Laser910 calls and says, pick you up at 9 a.m. and we will go and check out the Fire Bet at the Majestic Star in Gary, IN. We hadn't been there in awhile and were about to check out changes there anyhow.

We parked with a nice view of both boats frozen solid in ice. I told Laser he wouldn't have to worry about the boat rocking today. We went straight to Majestic Star II and found both tables closed. We crossed over to Majestic Star I and found one of the two tables open fully loaded with players.

We saw one of the brothers with three chip racks full of $100 chips ($30,000) playing from straight-out. He was betting $4,000 on the pass line, no odds. I said we got to watch this!

The point was nine and he put out a $4,000 come bet. It goes up on the six. He doesn't take any odds. Laser says this guy is crazy or just plain stupid. He loses both bets and then puts $4,000 on the PL again and gets a point of four and makes another come bet of $4,000. It goes up on the six again. Again he took no odds. The shooter makes the four and "brain dead" wins even money on the PL bet.

I told Laser that I can't watch this any longer. Let's see if they opened a table on the other boat. The crew was in place but they hadn't removed the plastic cover yet. We took up residence on both sides of the stick and Laser asked the crew how this fire bet works. One of the dealers went into great detail on explaining how it works. I had all I could do to keep from laughing. Laser probably knew more about the fire bet than the crew.

Before this charade went any further I said I have just one question. Can I have a chair? They laughed and there was a scramble to get the chair.

When we arrived there, we saw one of the suits sitting at the other table testing at least four sticks of dice for balance. When we finally got to play I noticed right away how sharp the dice were. My tosses were digging in but one die was going to the side a lot. If I would have got one more turn with dice I would have switched to the pincher grip.

The table was not bouncy to me and Laser wasn't having any bounce problems either. Both tables at MS II seemed to have new felt layouts. For 14 foot tables, I liked them.

We played for two and a half hours and everybody was making two or three points. Laser and I both threw C&E elevens after a craps number and a press. It was a good table of friendly players who were mostly senior citizens.

We were all set in our ways with Laser chasing the hard six and eight and me playing every shooter. The bottom line was we won more than enough to make up our losses last week at Joliet.

Oh yeah, a player from the other boat told Laser that "brain dead" was down to his last chip rack.

While I was cashing out, Laser come over and says the Suit wants to buy us dinner. East to the Lake is the only way to go.

Saturday Night at the Boat the Hard-way

Jan 20, 2008

"Saturday night at the Boat" could of been titled the "Night of the Hard-ways" or the Night of the "Happy Drunk" or the "Night of the Stupid Dice Pass" or the "Return of the Load Mouth" or just another "Saturday Night at the Boat with Laser".

We arrived at the dock and found the parking garage packed. So much for thinking the sub-zero weather would keep everybody home in front of the fireplace. It's been three weeks since we have been here on Saturday night and it was time to get back in the groove.

They had four tables working, There was a $10 and one $15. Of course our favorite table was the $15 table. We opted for the $10, 12 foot table that had openings at SR-2 and SL-2. My first mistake of the evening was not recognizing Mr. "Loud Mouth" at SR-1. He was jumping away from the table every time someone seven-out and cussing at nobody in general. After I seven-out he picked up his chips and left. There is a dice God after all.

With him gone I moved over to his spot at SR-1. Laser then opened up with a 3, 12, 11, and 7. Good start for our come out play on the C&E and pressing. We got loaded up just in time for the seven to bring us back to reality.

There was an unusual amount of hard-ways being thrown all night. Once I threw a hard six and Laser wasn't on it. He said do it again and he put ten on it. Dammed if I didn't throw another hard six! Now he felt better after missing the first one.

A happy go lucky drunk got the dice and was betting $5 on the 11 and 12. He hit the 12 and came right back with the 11. He was screaming at the top of his lungs every time it hit. Everybody was laughing at him and I was wondering if this was some of that table energy everybody is talking about. The guy was so slap happy drunk that the suits and security escorted him out of there and must have thrown him overboard.

We finally got a "Randy" that got on a roll. He was throwing six and eights like crazy. His problem was he had only a PL bet and a place bet on the five and nine. I didn't care what he threw because I had the "iron cross" set up and was collecting on everything. Then all of a sudden in this monster roll, he passes the dice and says to Laser, "I'm tired of throwing these Fu#@% six and eights for you as#@% holes" and walked away from the hand. Two throws later the guy he passed the dice to, threw a seven.

I said to Laser, "Can't you control your end of the boat."He said, "I guess not, but you got your own problems. Look who came back!" Mr. Load Mouth was back and on my right. He must have just come from the ATM machine. He bought in for $400 and said, "Come on, let's get going, I got to win back my money."

I had just got the dice and made two points when "jerko" say's, "Come on and make some numbers I got." He had all the hard-ways covered. I had been struggling all night trying to come up with a working set. I did something I never do. I set the hard-way set and let them fly. The throw was a good looking on-axis toss and came up seven.

Jerko was so upset he walked away from the table and started pacing back and forth mumbling something about my relations with my mother. When Laser and I colored up, I think there was smoke still coming out of his ears.

Once again Laser and I were the only one's tipping the dealers at that table. The dealers were especially attentive, setting the dice for us and reminding us of bets and presses. The suit provided our late evening snack and we jump the boat. We didn't even have to swim ashore. We ice skated back to the car. The temperature was -4 degrees.

Here We Go Again! Saturday Night at the Boat!

January 20, 2008

Here we go again, doing just what everybody tells us not to do. That's going to the Boat on Saturday night at prime time, 8 P.M.

Laser and I haven't hooked up since before Xmas and wanted to get in some action on the tables we will be playing on in the up coming Craps Tournament.

The Barge is packed and there are only two $10 tables open. We decided to go down and cruise the tables and wait for an opening. The Craps Gods must have returned from their coffee break because as we were approaching the second table, SL1 and SL2 open up. We jump in with a quick $300 buy in.

Surveying the table at first was discouraging. Not many chips in the racks and everybody very quite. Boy, were we in for a surprise. Laser says, "Cheer up Charlie; we never lose on Saturday night".

As we normally do, when just arriving at a table, we watched a young fellow in his early twenties come out. No bets. He tosses 7, 7, 11, and 10 for the point. I told Laser to watch what he was setting. Two rolls later he makes the 10. Laser says lets get on the band wagon. The young guy was using the X6's with the two, three up front on every roll. He had a beautiful soft toss.

We made our move on the PL with double odds and covered the inside numbers. Twenty minutes the kid kept making numbers. The sad part was that he only bet the PL with double odds.

His buddy got the dice next and low and behold, he was just as good. Set the dice (X6's) the same and had the same beautiful toss.

After one toss, we cover inside again and made one unit presses on each hit. He held the dice a good fifteen minutes.

The dice pass over to a third youth. Would you believe it!

They must have been triplets and cut from the same mold. Youth number three has the same toss and uses the same (X6's) set. He also had a fifteen minute run.

At this point a big lug of a guy was larking behind kid #3 and as soon as he seven-out, jump in next the kid to get the dice next.

I said to the stick girl, where did he come from? She said I saw that and then said something to the box-man. He shrugged his shoulders and they let him shoot.

Laser and I decided to stay off the big lug. What he did, bugged us. He was rewarded his justice real quick. He went 3, point 4 and 7-out. No chips lost on him.

The next shooter was a little guy who could hardly reach over the rail to make his bets or reach the dice. We were a little worried about him, but not for long. He was at SR2. He had a nice soft lob that hardly ever hit the back wall. No heat! But he did not set the dice! What was funny was twenty minutes into his roll he disappeared. Seems he had to go to the bathroom. What a night!

At this point I remarked to Laser, we have been here over one hour and a half and have not seen the dice. Laser says, "I'm up over $500, how you doing"? I remarked that we have our work cut out if we want hold up our end.

Meanwhile the guy at SR1 had taken over for the little guy going potty. I couldn't see what he was setting, but he was using the bowler grip and underhand toss.

He made a lot of numbers in his fifteen minutes plus.

Finally I got the dice! It was show time! What would the Captain do? Remember! Two games in one. I bet a $4 horn and doubling on the 3 and 11, $10 PL. For all my come outs I used my 5-6 set (5-6 on top and 6-5 front). The result was 3, 7, 11, 2, and 6 for the point. I made several passes including back to back ten's. Twenty minutes seem to be the norm when big red showed.

Now it was Laser's turn. I knew he was going to go hard-way crazy. He didn't disappoint us. It was a good hard-way table and they were turning up all over. I usually never play the hard-ways except on special occasions and this was one of them. We put another twenty minute roll on the board. What a boat ride and we haven't even gotten around the table with the dice.

The next four shooters were couples. The two girls made at least two passes and some numbers. We made money on them. Strangely the two fellows passed the dice. They were new to the game and were asking Laser a lot of questions.

Two older fellows rounded out the table. They both set the dice, using the stacked grip. They did alright but seem to have trouble with consistency, shooting from the hook next to the dealer.

That ended the first round and you couldn't ask for a better group to shoot with.

The second round was an image of the first round. The Craps Gods must have been right under our table. The only difference was Laser decided it was show time again. He went into the zone and didn't come out for over forty five minutes. At one point he parlayed a hard-way bet for the crew that resulted in a $90 win.

The newbie's asked why we were putting white chips along side our PL bets. Next thing you know they were doing the same thing. The crew made out big time.

Before Laser went into the zone, we had decided to pack it in after his roll. The only sour note of the boat ride was when one of the pit creatures announced that the table will now be $15. We were in the process of coloring out when he said it.

Weather the raise to $15 was intentional, I don't know. Why do it at 11P.M.? After we cashed in, we notice there were only six people left at our table.

While we were coloring out, the box-man thanked everybody for the tips and especially pointed at Laser and myself. What a boat ride!

Saturday Night at the Boat the Great Chip Spill

March, 2007

It could only happen on a crazy Saturday night at the Boat. Let me start from the beginning.

Saturday morning, on the golf course, Laser says lets hit the Majestic Star tonight. Target calls in the afternoon and has the same idea. It has been six weeks since the crew have been together for a Saturday night roll.

The tables at MS-1 were crowded so we went next store to MS-2 and found Target at SL2 at a $5 table. Some of the players recognized us and made room. The guy at SR1 was about to get the dice when he up and left. The stick asks me if I wanted to shoot before I even got my chips. This was great. Walk up to the table and they hand you the dice.

I threw the big red after about six tosses. Target wormed or charmed his way into SL1 and did the same thing. Laser (at SL2) also bombed on his first turn. We were all down about $150 by the time the dice got back to me.

Target had a profound look on his face and I told him to relax, were just getting warmed up. I got things rolling with a thirty minute run. Target batted next and was twenty minutes into his roll when it happened. The chip-fill! The floor Manager was putting six trays of red chips on the table when he dropped the whole batch of chips on the table wiping out all the bets on the 8, 9 and 10. The Suit, box-man, stick and dealer were all thumbs trying to re-stack everything.

In the process they knocked down more stacks of chips wiping out the 4 and 5 place bets. It really was comical. It took fifteen minutes to clear up the mess.

The three of us turned our bets off for Target's first roll after the spill. I told Target to keep focused and just get past that next roll. He threw a five and we turned on all our bets and he rolled for another fifteen minutes.

The suit was very apologetic and was yelling "yo-eleven" on Target's first roll after the chip spill.

We were not done. Laser proved why he is on the team with a twenty-five minute roll of his own. The Crew was back. We had three great hands in a row. We colored up, collected our $30 pizza comp and headed for shore. Was the spill intentional? I don't think so. There was too much panic in the crew to get things back to normal with the right bets in the right place. It makes you wonder though.

It might make for a good chapter in book 4, "THE GREAT CHIP SPILL." Well there you have it!

Charles C. Westcott

Saturday Night at the Boat, Foggy

April 21, 2008

On the way to the Boat Saturday night, Laser910 and I noticed fog banks over the Calumet River and lake. I remarked that we could have a problem coming home. Laser remarked that we had enough problems watching for pot holes let alone fog.

When we got to Majestic Star II, we found a parking spot over looking Lake Michigan but it wasn't there. We couldn't see the lake because of the fog. I said maybe that will cut down on the crowd tonight. The place was packed. Don't tell me there is a recession or the economy is bad! Not with all these people driving their high priced gas eating cars to the boat every night, eating, drinking and gambling like there's no tomorrow.

Once we maneuvered our way to the craps pit, we found a $15 table (12') with our spots open and only two other players there. The $10 tables were overflowing so we settled in on the $15 table. The dice were coming around fast and we were able to do a lot of shooting. This turned out to be a disadvantage over the long haul. Clubsodakenny checked in and we squeezed him into the flow that was going down hill fast. Clubsoda just missed Laser's opening hand when he went on a seven binge and threw in an eleven for good measure.

Playing at a $15 table with two other DI's and one Randy passing the Dice, it seemed like we had the dice all the time. It was hazardous to our bankroll when you figure you're playing a $15 PL with single odds, a $6 C&E and a $5 "fire bet" and then placing a $18 six and eight and don't forget $1 line bet for the crew. That's $60 or $78 in the game on each DI. It doesn't take many point sevens to demoralize you. We had plenty of them and felt we were spinning our wheels. I suggested we forget about the "fire bet" and see if we can find our way over to Resorts boat.

The five minute ride took a little longer with the fog. The parking garage was jammed. We ended up parking on the exit ramp and still no lake. The fog reminded me of that movie, "The Fog". If I see any pirates, I'm out of there. Again the casino was packed. Must be the good economy, the way people were tossing their money around. We had a little trouble finding the craps tables. I don't know what they got against craps players, or why they moved the tables to the back of the bus. Again the $10 tables were two deep. Laser found a spot at a $15 table and moved in

I stood around to the side of the stick watching this gentleman who was setting the V-3 and into a nice run. A friendly suit saw me and asked the fellow with the dice if I could squeeze in there next to the stick. Before he could answer I said I would wait until he finishes the hand so as not to jinx him. I figured he would cash out because his rack was over flowing. He made another point and a couple numbers and then seven-out.

He colored up for $1,018 and left. I knew what was going to happen next, after a long run like that. There was going to plenty of point sevens for awhile! There were eight, to be exact. We were down about four gas tank fill-ups and things were getting worse. For as much as we had the dice, we were stinking up the place. Laser said he was cashing in his pennies and would meet us at the Sports bar. Clubsoda was talking about jumping off the back of the boat. I said I was going "all in" with my remaining chips.

I threw three craps on the come out. I didn't press. Clubsoda says you're making $3 a throw. I then threw an eleven. That put $42 more dollars in the till. By now Laser was back and saw what was happening. I said you better get on me; we need fog money to get home. Laser jumps on the hard six. That was the point and I made it hard. Clubsoda changed his mind about jumping off the back of the boat and was fumbling in his pocket for more money. I told him, don't do it. Don't chase your money, it's too late. I made enough six and eights to ease the pain. I sevened-out three times but got the dice back because nobody else was at the table. I got $200 of my $400 buy-in back and was ready for the sports bar.

If Laser and Clubsoda had known I'd switched to the pincer grip and was using the Hard-way set for the point during that all-in roll, they would have thrown me of the boat.

Don't ask me how we got home, because we couldn't see anything with the fog. We didn't see any pirates either.

Saturday Night at the Boat Tornado

June 8, 2008

Saturday morning at the golf course, Laser910 says you know what tonight is. I said we better go to the Boat and check on the economy. It has been five weeks since we were there and we both had the itch in spite of all the tornados around us. I said it shouldn't be crowded with the Belmont race at 5:30 pm, the Sox at home and tornado warnings all around us.

Oh how wrong I was. The sky was blacker than soot and the black clouds were going right towards our destination. Half way there we got hit with heavy rain and had the windshield wipers working overtime. We chased the tornado clouds out into the lake and found a parking spot in a remote part of the parking garage that I never saw before. Laser says, "Too many cars, it's going to be over crowded."

Once inside it was a mass of humanity. All the slot machines were occupied with people waiting to for one to open up. The blackjack tables were packed with people waiting for a seat. We bump our way to the back of the boat where they had moved the Craps pit. Only three of the four tables were open. They had two twelve footers and one fourteen footer in play. All were $10 minimum tables.

The surprising thing was the two twelve footers were half empty and one of them had both our spots available. While buying in I noticed the guy at SR2 was about to get the dice. I barely got my chips and he passes the dice. This is great. Walked up to the table and get the dice! I showed my appreciation by going point seven and out. Laser responded the same way. In fact, nobody made a point in the first forty minutes. The dice were coming around fast with three bothers passing the dice.

We had two "Don't" players, one at the dealer hook and the other at SO. Laser said that the one at SO remarked, "Not those guys again," to no one in general. The next three times I had the dice, I made a point and then seven-out. Laser was struggling with his toss but then he made two quick points and Mr. SO was unhappy. When I got the dice again I noticed that Mr. SO was loading up on the "Don't" with $100 chips. Laser says, "Its show time, Charlie's got that look in his eye." No C&E bet this time. I set for the seven and threw it. Mr. SO loses his DP bet. I throw a ten for the point. Mr. SO is now is up on the DC ten. Two tosses later I make the ten. Mr. SO loses more of those $100 chips. Mr. SO stays off my next come out and I throw a three. Then I get five for the point and seven-out. Mr. SO colors up and leaves.

We never could get any sustained drives going. Laser decided to try the other twelve foot table, as his spot was open. He wasn't there long and decided to supplement his income on a five cent slot machine. I didn't want to leave the table we were on. I liked the way that my tosses were coming off the back wall and I thought conditions were good. When Laser left I even tried shooting from SL1. I was having a hard time getting past eight tosses. Most were six or less.

When shooting from SR1, this one healthy well stacked stick gal was blocking my view. When I moved to SL1 and got the dice, she was leaning way out with her fishing pole.

I thought I would scare her a little, but instead my back-hand follow through hit her stick into her forehead. The dealer suggested they get her a hard hat. However she did move back when I had the dice.

Another interesting occurrence was when a randy threw the dice and they only made it to the proposition area. That was a good six feet short of the back wall. The stick guy announced, "Six on a shorty." Nothing else was said.

If the economy is in such bad shape, where are all these gamblers getting the money to play with? I will say this. There is a lot of standing around at the tables.

The craps area is set up so it can be run by one suit. We had to ask the box person to find us a suit to get our comps. It ended up a non-profit Saturday Night at the boat. We both agree that we were suffering from lack of practice. The five week layoff showed.

Saturday Night at the Boat – New Digs

July 7, 2008

It had been a month now since we had been to the Boat. Sitting on the first tee, Laser910 says, "You feel like going to the Boat tonight? After all it's Saturday night." I remarked that it was time to check out what Ameristar has done since taking over from Resorts.

Laser910 says. "I'll pick you up around 6 p.m. and we will see if we can make enough money to pay for the gas. On the way there, Laser gets a call from his son Radar. Radar tells Laser to bet the five and nines. He said he had a feeling that the five and nines were going to be hot.

We find a good parking spot and Laser says that's a good sign. Once inside we could see the changes they were making. New walls going up and the relocation of the table games made a lot of sense. You now had room to get to the cashier cage without bumping into the craps shooters. The craps pit was moved to the rear of the room but allowed more space for the players at the tables.

There are four tables, two 14 footers and two 12 footers. All have new felt layouts with a nice area for keeping track of the Hoping Sevens bet. No Fire bet! There was two $10 and two $15 tables and all were in play. 100xodds.

There were openings at all four tables. We circled the tables a couple of times and settled for 12 footer with a $10 minimum. Laser was at SL1 and I settled for SR2. We noted that some of our favorite dealers were scattered throughout the other tables. I recognized two of the Suits. A big tall dude recognized me from the last time we were there and asked if I was going to shoot the dice tonight. I said I would give it a try.

After buying in, the cat shooting from the dealer hook established five for the point and came right back with a five. He comes out again and gets five for the point and came right back with a five. He throws a nine and then hits his five again. I look at Laser and he looks at me. Now I'm not a believer in a metaphysical plane or physic sensory sixth sense but Radar's intuition or divine knowledge makes you wonder.

It was time for us to participate in this unusual behavior of the dice being thrown by a random shooter who was setting the V-3 and flinging the dice as hard as he could to the wall. Fifty percent of his throws were bouncing of the table. This went on for a good twenty minutes and got us off to a good start.

The next three shooters had the same problem of keeping the dice on the table. They held the dice for a long time but their results weren't very good. Most of their time with the dice was spent with the box guy checking the one that flew off the table and they kept saying "same dice."

When I finally got the dice I kept them low and slow to go. What surprised me was the recoil off the rubber baby bumpers on the back wall. The dice were coming back off the wall to the prop bets area. I tried to dribble the dice into the back wall. They still would bounce weirdly. I finally made three passes and some numbers using a permutation of the V-3 and concentrated on just making a good toss. The dice were going all over the place and I knew I was getting nothing but random results.

Laser was having the same problem and didn't get going until his last roll. Prior to that, he was living off the hard sixes.

The location of the craps tables are good. The personnel are good. No heat what so ever. The Suits paid no attention to us with one exception. When I was into my one good roll, the female Suit watch one toss and then smiled and walked away. These tables are going to drive a lot of DI's to drink. It's a shame because the place is becoming a class act.

After two hours of play, Laser suggested we jump ship with a profit and call it a lucky Saturday night at the Boat. Maybe next time we will listen to Radar's divine intuition.

Saturday Night at the Boat - They Love Us

July 14, 2008

Saturday night we arrived at the tables at 8 pm. This particular Boat has four twelve foot tables, all $10. All four tables were open. One table was full and another had four players with SR and SL both open. The third and forth tables were empty. All these choices, what's a guy suppose to do.

We circled the tables a couple of times and finally decided on the empty table closest to the cashier's cage with the blond stick gal and the good looking box gal. The emptiness must be due to the Memorial Day weekend.

Laser got the dice first and had a quick seven out. My turn was a little better, getting 17 tosses in. Laser followed with a decent hand and the dice were back in my hand. After a come out three I pressed the C & E to $12 and came right back with an eleven. $84 in the tray and we were off and running. Two come out sevens and finally a point of six. Before making the six I tossed four fours.

Next thing I know, there are six CF's at the table and things slowed down to a crawl. The CF's were coming out of the woodwork or from under the carpet. Trying to catch a hot CF can be very hazardous to your bankroll. We played at that table for two hours and were just about even. We had the only sustained rolls at that table.

Laser suggested we move to the other empty table. Chips in hand we moved. Laser opened with a good roll of fifteen or better. Next thing I know this table is getting full. I mentioned to Laser that the same faces are back at this table. Laser said yeah, they are following us again and they don't have the brains to pass the dice.

During the hour we were at that table, the stick guy related to Laser that the crews like dice setters because they attract people to the tables and they bet more while making the time go faster by keeping them busy. He said we make more points and attack more betting.

Later one of the other stick guys asked me if I took lessons from GTC. I said no, but I know a couple of losers who did. The stick guy thought that was funny. Here I thought that GTC meant "Great Toss Charlie."

During the three hour session, I was up a hundred or down a hundred and broke out even. Laser lost a couple chips.

When we left the table everybody turned around to see if we were going to another table. We hit the cashier's cage and headed towards the parking garage. Laser looked around and said, "Well, they are not following us to the car". I said that we probably lost them when we stopped at the men's room.

Saturday Night at the Boat – Overview

August 4, 2008

Clubsodakenny calls and says its time we check out all the boat rehabbing going on at the lake front and cash in some coupons. It has been about a month since Laser910 and I had made the dice scene. This trip we gave Laser the night off to attend to some family business.

With Clubsodakenny at the wheel, we had no trouble finding a place to park at the Majestic Star. It wasn't crowded and there wasn't that mass of humanity moving back and forth among the slot machines. The two fourteen foot craps tables were packed. Both were $5 minimum tables. Clubsoda spotted a craps table set off to the side. I swear it was a ten footer. If they put that table into play, we will have to check it out in the future. It looks like they were making an effort to clean the place up and were moving things around.

We cashed our coupons and headed over to Ameristar. Ameristar was more active than MS and had more renovations in progress. When Harrah's owned it, it was fair but had bouncy tables. Resorts took over and made some improvements and there seemed to be less smoke. We also became adjusted to one of their tables and had many good Saturday nights on it. Ameristar now owns it and has made more improvements. They moved the craps tables to the rear of the boat where there is more room and you are not back up against the cashier's cage rubbing butts with the winners.

Our positions at the tables were all filled with Randies and our favorite table was a $15 minimum and no openings. We decided to head over to the new Horseshoe.

Clubsoda noted that we were $70 ahead and hadn't even thrown the dice yet. I said that we would have to test the water at the Horseshoe.

We ended up parking on the sixth floor. The place was packed. Now I knew why our first two stops were lacking the usually big Saturday night crowds. They were all at the Horseshoe. Boy! Is the place big! The casino area is bigger than anything I've ever seen in Vegas. I tried comparing it with Wynn, Venetian and others. The Horseshoe is bigger and just as classy.

I remarked to Clubsoda that there were only four craps tables. He said, look again. They are six more over there. They actually had two craps pits. I thought I was in Craps heaven, ten tables. They were all staffed and working. Most of the tables were $10 minimum. There was a $15 and $25 table.

We got position and jumped in a $10 table. A Randy was on a roll and I watched him make a couple points after buying in. How did we know he was going to stay hot? We were the new kids on the block and didn't want to get caught with our hand in the cookie jar. There were some quick seven-outs and I finally got the dice. I got nine for my point and came right back and made the nine and then went point seven out. It was the only time I got to throw the dice.

It was very noticeable that every one else was throwing the dice off the table but I will reserve any conclusions about the tables till I can play on them more.

The crew was OK but the Box Guy was super. A real friendly person and talked with everybody. It was a boat trip that needs further investigation.

Saturday Night at the Boat,
New Horseshoe Revisited

August 17, 2008

Laser910 and I arrived on the forth floor of the parking garage around 6:15 pm and found a parking spot not to far from the elevator. Laser910 remarked that this could be a lucky night. The casino was nowhere as crowded as last weekend. There were plenty of people there but the place is so big they were lost in the hugeness of the place.

There were plenty of slot machines available for play (3200). The over 100 table games were pretty much filled up. Their restaurants were just like Vegas, wait in line.

Eventually we found the ten craps tables which were all manned and we settled into a table that had our spots open. It was the same table I played on last week. Next to it was the same reserved table as last week, with one player at it. Our table was a $10 minimum, 12 footer with100Xodds.

The Suits were friendly with one exception when the one Suit fired our player's cards back across the table. I ended up with Target's card and he with mine. Target and Clubsodakenny had just joined us at the table and we now had murders row set up with two of us on each side of the stick person.

The table was choppy and according to Clubsoda we were averaging 12 to14 tosses each on our rolls. It wasn't enough to compensate for the Randies wild tosses. One Randy threw the dice off the table five straight times and then went seven out. All of us were approaching our stop loss figure when Laser and Target decided to hit the video poker machines. Clubsoda and I decided to throw the dice one more time and then take a break.

We where walking around taking in the casino when we spotted Analomys at a 14 foot table in the second craps pit. He had his book and pen out and was busy at work at SL1. He had a serious amount of chips in front of him and we didn't want to disturb him while a happy go lucky Randy was having a hot roll from SO. SR1 opened up for about twenty seconds and I hesitated jumping in.

You snooze, you lose! I didn't want to upset the flow of the game with a buy in the middle of the run, which lasted a good twenty-five minutes.

Target and Laser found us watching the action. Now the whole crew was standing behind Analomyst watching the action. Finally there was a break in the action and we all got to meet and shack hands with Analomyst. We told him we were going to get something to eat and try to get back to his table.

After filling our stomachs we decide to go to our home base, Ameristar and try to recoup our losses. We had a short meeting in the washroom, washed our hands and headed to our favorite table. Laser and Clubsoda jumped into their spots, SL1and 2 and Target and I were at SR2 and SR3.

The guy next to Target had the dice and was having a little run. Target jumped in fast to get a bet down on the pass line because he was to get the dice next. I used Target's move to buy in also. Target and I had mini rolls and then Laser got serious and had the best run of the night. All four of us at one time or another threw come out elevens. We recouped a good part of our previous losses.

It was a relief to get back to a good table crew. The female suit even walked around the table to give us our player's cards. Again at both boats, we were the only one's betting for the crew. It paid off on some close calls.

Saturday Night at the Boat –
The Good, Bad and Ugly

Aug. 31, 2008

We have got a new route to the Horseshoe Boat that takes twenty-four minutes to travel twelve and a half miles from my front door. That's **good!**

Once you get to the parking garage you are faced with the steepest inclines to reach the upper floors to park. That's **bad!**

It's one long walk to the elevator and a longer walk to the Craps area. That's **bad!**

I still marvel at the vastness of the place. The various places to eat require you to take an elevator and there seems to be a big wait just to get one. That's **bad!**

The cashier's cage caters to the second and third level player's card holders. There were seven windows open for the preferred players and only one for us low rollers. I guess I will have to gamble more. That's **bad!**

Finally we got to the tables and they were packed with humanity. They had ten tables and only two $10 minimums. Two of the ten were reserved for those invisible players. That's **bad!** We went and stood behind SR1 and SL1 at a $10, fourteen foot table. Ten minutes later we were in position with seven other Angelo Saxon and three Afro-American voters. Laser got to throw twice and I threw once. Table was ice cold and we couldn't get enough throwing time to change it. That's bad! What made it worse was the table crew was inexperienced, slow and couldn't add. That was **ugly!**

Laser said he had enough and headed to the poker machines. I agreed and followed him. Video poker took us for a ride and that was **ugly**! I suggested we go over to Ameristar, seven miles and ten minutes away.

We had no trouble parking and found the casino empty. They only had two of the four craps tables open. Both were $10 and filled with players. Laser headed for the poker machines. I spotted an opening at SL1 and jumped in. The table crew was good and friendly and I knew the suit. By the time I got the dice, the table had emptied and there were only three of us left. All the point sevens cleared everybody out. It got worse. I found myself the only one left.

I played for a half hour on a Saturday night, all by myself. That was **good!** The results were ugly. I have never thrown so many sevens in my life. I would throw two sevens on the come out, get a point and seven out. No matter what I set on the come out, I would throw two or three sevens and then point seven and out. Boy was it **ugly**! It was so **ugly** that the suit gave me a $50 comp for food. I took it and ran.

I found Laser busy recouping some of his loses and said lets go eat our troubles away. I told Laser it must have been those blue dice. Thinking back on it now, playing the hopping sevens might have been the answer.

It was a Saturday night we both would like to forget.

Saturday Night at the Boat, 2009

January 4, 2009

It had been three weeks since the crew found their way back to the big U on the lake. With the holidays out of the way, it was time to get back in the toss of things. After the beating we took at the "Grand Victim" (Victoria), we wanted to get back to the friendly confines of Lake Michigan's boats.

As what has become a routine for us, we went looking for trouble. You might say we were testing the water after all the weird stuff that has been reported lately. I guess we just like to do everything the "Hard-way", playing on a Saturday night at prime time, at 7:30 pm. We thought the place was going to be packed by the way the parking garage was loaded. To our surprise, there were openings at just about all of the nine out ten tables working.

We found Target camped at one of the $10, twelve foot tables playing in my position. Laser910 says let's jump on the empty table next to the one Target was at. We picked out the table that has been giving us fits the last couple times out. The table is like a magnet. It draws us to it more than any of the other tables. The table crew is the best and the suits are friendly. I was given a chair before I had time to buy in. The table had the Fire Bet and nobody cared about the back wall.

The only comment during the two hours of play was when one of a Randy's tosses only made it half way down the layout. All that was said by the stick was, "point is six on a shorty." When ever we are on that table we have a hard time leaving it. Target was struggling and threatening to go home. Laser910 went looking for his check book. I was wondering where $400 went. We finally headed for the video poker machines for a break.

Target donated some more green backs to the casino boat economy and Laser910 was hard at work recouping some of his losses. I went back to the tables and found my spot at the private table open with the dice two players away. I was tossing the dice with confidence all night; running twelve to twenty throws a hand.

I was just giving too much back on everybody else. You can lead a craps player to the table but you can't make him leave it.

I noticed there wasn't any Fire Bet on this table and ask why. Their answer was they just don't want it on the reserve tables. My next surprise came when they change to a $15 table and I went to make a $6 C&E bet and was told it had to be a $10 bet. I said OK; make it a $12 C&E. I threw a three for a $36 payoff and pressed up to $24 and threw another three. No elevens all night!

I established ten for the point and put out $10 odds and was told it had to be $15. I played dumb and asked if it was OK to put $20 odds on my $15 PL bet. They said yes. I put another chip on the odds for the crew and shortly made the ten after making a bunch of five, six, and eights. Every time I made a point the box guy clapped. He kept thanking me for the bets. I told him, I should be thanking you. You people are forcing me to win more money.

It was my best roll of the night and Laser910 got in on the tail end. Target had already jumped ship and missed the boat. CSK, you should have been there. It beats painting!

One thing that was of interest was I was purposely setting slow and letting Target and Laser see what I set. The other players at the table were polite and were enjoying the moment. The table crew wasn't about to say anything and were very appreciative of the tokes.

We stayed for one more roll, colored up and spent the next twenty eight minutes coming home.

It's time to take a boat break......

Chapter 37

Are We Good for Craps?

Are we as dice setting advantage players good for the game of craps and the casinos in general? I think we are. More and more people are being exposed to craps in many ways. The dice seminars are attracting people who are just about willing to pay anything to learn the game as we play it.

If this were not true, then why are monthly income percentage comparisons at the craps tables higher than other table games and slots? The economy is throwing things out of sync but still there is the demand to learn more about the game. The interest in craps has picked up do to the fact that there are vehicles out there to increase one's knowledge like seminars, web sites, individual instructors and more books.

In the past the only way you could learn how to play craps was to read a book or watch someone else play. Books never tell you the whole story. I know, I wrote three of them. As soon as I published one, I would discover something I left out or new concepts would come to light. Casino's sometimes stage lessons on the basics of craps but nothing of substance like you find on the Dice Institute web site.

More and more people are being exposed to craps everyday because of us. They watch us play and often ask us where we learned how to shoot like that. They try to copy our play and watch us set the dice. So they set the dice because they think that's what you have to do or they are just trying to look like they know what their doing.

We tend to draw more players to the table when they see us roll. These players will sit on the side lines or follow us around to see what table we will play at. Players will stay at a table longer than they should, just to be there when it is our turn to roll. We defiantly draw a crowd when we get hot. Players will bet more on our rolls.

Some casinos realize when we are at the table the crew is going to make plenty of tokes. We tend to keep players at the table longer. Yes, I would say we are good for the casinos. We are doing their job promoting the game. We are the only one's promoting the game, teaching the game and making people aware of the pros and con's of the game. It's too bad all the casinos don't realize what an asset we are to the game.

Chapter 38

The "Five Count" Revisited

Is the "**Five Count**" a viable system to be used by the dice influencer? Can the **"Five Count"** be used in advantage play?

There is a segment of the dice community that still believes in the system. In short, they feel that if 50% of the shooters are expected to seven-out before the sixth roll of the dice, they are saving money by not betting till the sixth roll.

They also contend that the first and last number of the "**Five Count**" should be a box number. So that means if the first or last number is a 2, 3, 11, or 12, your actual count will really be six or seven or eight count.

When you reach their count of five, you are told to put a come bet out. The theory is that the seven is expected on the next roll. If the seven doesn't show, the come bet goes to a box number and you put another come bet out. You stop "come" betting after three "come" bets.

Here's where the system falls apart. After their count of five the expectancy of the seven increases while they continue to put chips in jeopardy. Some theory! They are trying to catch a hot roller after he has put six or more numbers on the board. That's a sure waste of good numbers.

Here's where the dice influencer comes in. He uses the **"Reverse Count."** He's got the dice and bets the pass line. After establishing a point, he places the six and eight and takes odds on his pass line bet. He throws four more times and pulls down all his bets except the pass line. What he has done is to remove his bets during jeopardy time after five rolls.

Regression betting is ideal for the **"Reverse Five Count"**. Spread betting will work also. Stay away from the come betting. If you have a SRR of 8.0, jump in right away. When that eighth roll comes up, run for cover.

What I don't understand in this day and age of dice setting and influencing, is why the out dated "Five Count" system is still being taught! The "Captain" should be made to walk the plank.

Chapter 39

Turn It Off or Take It Down?

Turning off or taking down your bets is one of the hardest strategies to master. The thing you have to decide is how many winners you need just to break even by staying up.

Let's say you have about $250 on board and in the zone, when on your next toss, one die misses the back wall. The box guy gets on your case and tells you to hit the back wall or else. This upsets you and you throw a couple junk numbers. The thought crosses your mind to turn off all your bets. That, in it self would be a good move, considering you lost your rhythm and were throwing junk numbers. To prevent any mistakes and losing that amount, it might have been better to take down all your bets instead of turning them off.

I never turn off a bet. I prefer to come all the way down and get my chips off the table. Trying to out guess yourself weather you can get back in the zone is impossible. You already made a bunch so far and you were getting a signal that all was not well. You were upset and the Box was on your case.

When the thought of jumping ship enters your mind, listen to that guy that resides between your ears and pull out and stay out. In the long run, you will never have to worry about that happening again. Think about it. You have all the inside numbers covered and a sizable odds bet behind your pass line bet. How many hits do you need to cover all that exposure? In your condition, can you do it? Take the money and run. If you turn everything on and seven-out, you will really go on tilt. Not hitting the back wall is a common problem we all have to learn to live with the ramifications that occur whether we hit the wall or not. When this over zealous box guy jumped on you, you could have retorted in a nice friendly manner, "Gee, I'm terribly sorry, I'll try to do better". This immediately defuses the situation and takes the thunder out of the box guy. As it turned out, he accomplished his goal and upset you in the middle of a roll.

My advice to any DI is to defuse the situation. Get the crew on your side and enjoy the game, don't fight it.

Chapter 40

How I got started in Dice Influencing

The question I get most is why did I write four books on craps? Boredom is the answer. During the three winter months when I can't be out on the golf course, I get cabin fever.

I used those winter months to read dozens of craps books. I have always loved craps and after reading all those books, I came to the conclusion that most of them said the same thing. I used some computer results to prove some of those expert's offerings. I thought it would be interesting to put the best of all their ideas together in one book. Enter book one.

"CRAPSHOOTERS WAKE UP AND SMELL THE ROSES" was put together on 67 pages. That doesn't say much for the experts, but then they were playing the same strategy for thousands of years. The book was for the average craps player who was tired of missing out on the big roll because his bankroll was gone before it happened. The time frame was 2001.

Then came the winter of 2002! What to do! It's hell being retired. I got to thinking about the beginner who knew nothing about the game and was scared to death to try it. He needed something more than just the basics. Enter Book two. *"CRAPS AND SMELLING THE ROSES"* is a good read for the beginner and the guy who thinks he knows it all. You are given a guided tour of the game of craps from the moment you walk in the casino door until you exit the cashier's cage. It includes everything that was in book one and 50% more. It has 116 pages of easy to understand craps jargon.

Just after Book two was released, I was taken in by PARR and Sharpshooter's book. A new world was opening up. Dice setting! The Rest of 2002 and 2003 were spent practicing what Sharpshooter's book was expounding on. Then GTC popped up. Somewhere along the way, one night at the Boat, Target say's, "hey Charlie, you got to check out the web site called Irishsetter.com." This was coming from a guy who was schooled by GTC twice.

In 2004 I checked out the site and was active on it till December of 2005. I got the winter book-writing urge to do one final book. This book would start where all the other books left off. No basics. If they need basics, they can read book two, first.

In 2006 I saw two books about to come out. "The Mad Professor's Shooting Bible" and my *"WAKE UP CRAPS SHOOTERS and Join the Dice Revolution"*. Both books should give you the same result but are presented in different ways.

"WAKE UP CRAPS SHOOTERS" is a step by step manual on how to accomplish what the casinos say can't be done. Dice Influencing!

The book is for experienced craps shooters who want to dedicate themselves to the modern way of playing craps.

The release date was April 19, 2006 and can be bought through Amazon Books. I don't write books for a living and have tried not to push any books on anybody. I do it for the enjoyment I get out of helping someone else succeed at craps.

Since late 2005 till now, dice related web sites have come to the fore front and have become a great source of craps information.

In late 2006 Dead Cat and I created the Private Members Forum and in February, 2007 we went on the internet with Dice Institute. com. Dice Institute.com has become the largest free source of dice influencing, control, skilled, precision shooting anywhere.

Getting started on this journey was an accumulation of ten years of studying the game of craps, attending seminars and spending many Saturday nights at the casino boats. The long hours of practice was rewarding and has paid off in dividends

Two and a half years ago I started accumulating this mass amount of dice information and decided that the only place for it was in Book #4. All the adventures at the casino boats are lessons in themselves.

Teaching craps came by accident. A neighbor of mine heard I just got back from Vegas and was going and wanted some advice on craps. He said he loves the excitement of the game but has never won at it. My first book had just come out and I got him a copy and invited him to come over and we would discuss the game.

We spent an hour and a half discussing money management and some simple bets. He brought a note pad with him and took notes as we talked. He said he had read the book and had some questions. From the questions he was asking, I could see that there was a need for a beginner's book.

When he returned from Vegas he said it was the first tine he has ever won at craps. It wasn't much, but it was a win.

When my second book aimed at beginners, came out it was already obsolete with the emergence of dice setting on the scene. Book #3 would be my last book and cut right to the chase. No basics, just an easy book to read on dice setting. One premiere player said he read it on the plane and said he couldn't wait to get to the tables. Another player said he started to read it at night in his hotel room and couldn't put it down till he finished it. Another player said why don't you put all three books together and cover all bases.

I think I went one step further and have the basics covered, dice setting and influencing the dice and went over every possible problem or situation that can come up in the game. The adventures at the boat casinos are factual and not fiction. Hopefully this book will serve as an answer to any problem that might rise up in a game of craps.

Before DS and After DS

Before **D**ice **S**etting came on the scene you had the old school of thinking which included a pass line bet with odds and two come bets. This was pretty much advocated by most of the gambling authors until Frank S. came out with the "Five Count."

I used it and described it in book one with the "Wait and Fire" method of play. As soon as book one came out, a whole new conception of play hit the dice community. Dice setting was the new rage and just about everybody was setting in some fashion or other. My book two was obsolete before the ink dried. It was however a good book for beginners.

After DS I saw a need for book three. This was a whole new ball game. There was a quick need for a simple book explaining dice setting and the advantages of learning the new concept of advantage play.

If you have managed to get this far in this book you can see that there is a lot more to this game of craps than meets the eye. It has become a never ending journey of enhancing you're craps ability.

Chapter 41

Energy from the Table Crew

The way we are treated by the table crew and pit plays one of the most important parts in selecting a place to play. I rate it above table size, bounce and $ minimum.

It makes you feel real good when the Suit comes over and greets you with a Hi, glad to have you back, where you been?

Or; the box guy says, Hi Charlie, you want a chair tonight?

Or; one of the dealers says; OK, now we got a shooter at the table.

Or; the stick person asks the guy at SR1 to move so you can have your preferred position.

Or; the cute little female dealer says, we missed you and your friends.

Or; the stick person says, come on Mr. C, make that ten.

When coloring up, the Suit says, do you want your pizza tonight?

Under these conditions, you experienced a warm feeling even though you might have had a losing session.

Chapter 42

Respect for the Box Person

Over the years I have learned to appreciate the box person position. I use to think the box person was nothing but a suit in training. Now that I am playing more often, I have witnessed the box person intervene in payouts and the placing of bets. Their job becomes even harder when breaking in a new dealer or putting up with burned out dealers.

How often have you seen the stickman have trouble paying off C & E, horn and world bets? The good box person jump right in and tell the stick how much to pay. I have even seen the box person take over for a new dealer just to keep the game moving along.

One time I was shorted two red chips and before I could say anything, the box person told the dealer to pay me two more red chips. Another time my place bet was placed in the wrong position in the box. Just as I was to say something, the box person reached over and put the bet in the proper place.

When you play from SR like I do, you are right across from the box person and have a lot of eye contact with him. That's the time to get him on your side with some casual comment.

Then there is the box person who looks like he's falling asleep. When you run into him you better hope the dealers are on the ball and the cameras are rolling.

Chapter 43

Record Keeping and What is SRR?

There are so many web sites out there with so much loose information, that a person can go blind trying to digest it all.

What is the philosophy behind the SRR? Sevens to Roll Ratio is a great training tool. Nobody likes to practice unless they can show a result. The SRR is figured by dividing your number of tosses by the number of sevens you throw. The result is your SRR.

If you throw the dice 36 times which includes 6 sevens, you have a SRR of 6.0. If you throw 7 sevens, you have a SRR of 5.14. That's below the average bear. Now if you throw 5 sevens within 36 tosses, you will have an SRR of 7.2. That's all you need to tip the casino advantage to your favor. If you only throw 4 sevens in 36 tosses, you will be better than me.

The results tell you what sets will work for you. It gives you your signature number. It tells you how fewer sevens you are throwing. You can see how good you are rolling over any amount of time such as 36, 100, 200, 500 etc rolls.

What does it tell me? It tells me that I am a solid SRR of 8.15 over 50,640 rolls. It tells me that I only rolled 6,205 sevens. It tells me that I rolled 2,235 less than expected 8,440 sevens.

Regression can cause a depression. For the most part I think that a good many players can't afford to play some of the regression systems suggested. If you can over come a SRR of 8 on a $5 table, you would have $44 inside waiting to come down to $22. You need at lest two hits to show a small profit. Knowing your SRR Will help you decide when to come down. A $10 table is double the exposure.

I would agree that regression is counter productive under any conditions unless you reach a stage in the game where you have pressed up after getting your seed money out of the game.

The only way to find out if you are progressing as a Dice Influencer is to keep detailed records. You will need a practice station or table. You also will need a chart to record your practice tosses. A pair of regulation dice is a must (.075).

This is what dice influencing is all about. Keeping good records will help tell you when your are ready to step up to the casino tables and play craps with the knowledge of what is the best play for you.

The next page is an example of the chart I use to keep track of all my practice throws. It has five columns of thirty-six for a total of 180 rolls per page.

009 Practice Form   Date_____

SRR_____	SRR_____	SRR_____	SRR_____	SRR_____
Dice Set_____	Dice Set_____	Dice Set_____	Dice Set_____	Dice Set_____

7's*	Pairs	Remks.	7's*	Pairs	Remks.	7's*	Pairs	Remks.	7's*	Pairs	Remks.	7's*	Pairs	Remrks.

Total Rolls_____   Total 7's*_____   Total Rolls_____   Total 7's*_____

Current SRR_____   On Going SSR_____

Chapter 44

Good throws...Bad throws...

When your throw is off, no matter how much skill you have, you have to have the knowledge or patience to correct the problem.

Most of the players we run into are lacking the knowledge this book provides.

You ask whether poorly executed dice influencing can result in more sevens than randomly expected! It all depends on how we look at influencing.

Most of us are usually a little off axis 50% of the time. Does that mean we are negatively influencing the dice when we are off axis? I don't think so! The DI's, who are too lazy to practice and gain Craps Knowledge, are still just random shooters. When a practiced DI is off axis a little, he is still going to get better than random results. Is there anyone out there that has less than SRR of 6.1?

To answer the question, a little knowledge with out follow up training can be dangerous. Take for instance the DI who uses the Hard-way set and he keeps throwing sevens, it's obvious that he is "double pitching" with that set and doesn't have the knowledge to correct it. In this case there would be more sevens than random. I rest your case!

A knowledgeable skilled DI would take measures to correct his problem. If that fails, he would switch to the dark side or exit door right. Like they say, it's "Knowing when to hold them and knowing when to throw them!"

There are times when taking a break from craps is the only solution to a bad run at tables. There also are times when your shooting mechanics seem okay but your decision making process goes on strike.

Playing craps is like walking through a mine field without a mine detector. Some of the mines are concentrated in the middle of the table. Watch your step!

Most of the mines will be set up on the pass line in the form of chips bet along the back wall where you're landing zone is. Learn to live with it. You just can't say, *"Move those dam chips!"* Well you might as well be blunt about it if you are going to say anything. You might as well just announce to everybody that you are a dice influencer and you need a clear path to the back wall. You are a marked player from that time on and will bear watching.

I never could hit anything I was aiming at, so when there are chips in my landing zone I aim right at them. They dice usually split with one die going on one side of the chips and the other going on the other side.

I demonstrated this shot At Dicecoach's at Spring Fling and was accused of doing trick shots.

If there are chips in your way, go around them or over them or go right at them, like I do. Try it in practice and you will be surprised how hard it is to hit a stack of chips. It's time we got back to flying under the radar.

Chapter 45

Quantum Slump?

Was I in a quantum slump or was I just making mistakes at the tables?

For the past month I have been in a quantum slump of my own doing. My last three visits to the Boats have resulted in losses. My practice sessions have been just as bad. I can't seem to get past eight rolls. My perfect on axis toss (when I get one) has resulted in too many sevens.

I finally decided to try and analyze every move I made in the last month. We have been taught to do what we know to do.

The first Boat loss was when I played too much on other DI's that were in town, without qualifying them. There were enough of us at the table that we didn't need to put action on the CF's. That was a bad mistake!

The second Boat loss, everything was out of sync. After buying in, I stood there with chips in my hand and watched a CF throw some fifteen numbers. When one CF had six for the point, the little voice in my head said, "Play the hard six." I ignored the thought and watch the next toss come up hard six. I can remember at least three other times during that session that I ignored that little voice and went down in flames. To top it off, I was at the same table as the Kooler.

He threw just enough numbers for me to set up the Iron Cross and then seven-out. I have got to listen to that little voice.

That brings us to my last Boat outing. This mistake was simple. I just refused to go to the dark side and play the Don't. The dice went completely around the full table with no one making a point. If Golfer would have been there, he would have owned the Boat. I've learned my lesson, Dark side here I come.

As far as practicing is concerned, I quit messing with the sets and have concentrated on the toss. When I use the same set for 72 rolls, I seem to throw too many sevens. When I set for the point or chase the point I seem to have longer runs.

Mad Professor, where were you when I needed you? I took your advice and had a martini, changed to green dice, put on a baseball hat backwards, said three hail Mary's and started doing what comes naturally.

It's a matter of doing what we know to do for a quantum fix.

Chapter 46

ABC's of Practice

Advantage play in craps can only be gained by hours of dedicated practice, learning the necessary skills to overcome the casino's advantage.

Betting scenarios should be tried at home in practice before making bets in the real world of casino wagering.

Come-out plays a strategic part of your game within a game strategy. Incorporate it into your practice sessions.

Dice setting will gain you an advantage over the seven. If you throw just one less seven in thirty six rolls than the expected six, you gain a slight advantage over the casinos.

Even money pass-line wager is the best bet when accompanied with an odds bet. Mock wagering on your practice layout well help you gain confidence on the bet when trying to throw a seven on the come-out.

Field bets are not recommended percentage plays, but can be used in iron cross play. The strategy should be worked out in practice before trying it.

Grips of various styles should be tried until you find one that suits you and is comfortable to your physical needs.

Hard-ways are a negative percentage play that is not recommended. You should use the hard-way set in practice to see how many primary numbers you are throwing.

Influencing the dice is our ultimate goal. The only way we will accomplish this is by establishing good practice habits.

Join the member's message forum to get the answers to your needs on gaining the skills necessary to influence the dice.

Keep records to determine your progress and skill level and determine your signature number.

Learn the various bets on the table layout and work them into your practice sessions. Learn what you want to do before you try it in the casino.

Muscle memory should be a part of your craps arsenal, once you have developed your toss skill.

Numbers is what we want to throw. We don't care what numbers, just so it's not a seven. Remember as long as it is not a seven, we still control the dice. Keep track of the number of tosses between sevens.

On axis is what we want to throw every toss. Only regular practice will develop the skill necessary to keep the dice on axis.

Practice, practice, practice, practice and then practice some more. It is the only way to have a chance at influencing the dice.

Quick setting will have to be practiced and mastered if you are going to stay out from under the watchful eyes of the casino personnel.

Real casino play should not be attempted until you have developed the necessary skills and confidence to enhance your chances of winning.

Shooting the dice properly from start to release point should become second nature to you. Check out the grip section. The toss is one of the most important parts in dice control.

Table to practice on is a must, weather it's a practice rig you made or bought, or a pool table, or even the real thing. You should have the standard layout, chips and a supply of different colored dice.

Use new dice. Dice will wear and the edges will become dull and chipped. Only practice with casino approved dice to maintain close to casino conditions.

V-2 and V-3 sets should be used in practice and mastered before going live in the casino. These two sets have only two expected sevens and are favored by most DI's.

Winning comes with self control. Losing comes with no self control. Self control means betting only money you can afford to lose. No self control is when you over extend your wagering and bankroll.

X-6's is another good set with only two expected sevens. Use it in practice and see if it fits into your game plan.

Your set, grip, release point and toss are the most import parts of the A, B, C's of advantage play and dice influencing. Learn them well.

Zone is the place you want to be in. Hitting your target zone with your toss is one thing but when you put it all together and get into the zone at the craps table and make number after number, its second heaven.

Chapter 47

The Dice Community As I Know It

Over the past ten years I have had the privilege of meeting and playing with some of the finest people in the dice community. They are the cream of the craps world and can be consider the all-stars of the game.

The **Target,** a GTC trained player and one of the original boat crew members, put me onto **Irishsetter's** web site. It was through his member's forum I learned of **Heavy's** seminar and attended. I met **Dice Coach** at that time and soon realize what a good dice instructor he was. If you need a tune up I would recommend you see the **Dice Coach** when you are in Las Vegas.

Maddog is to be commended for the contribution of his Bone Tracker program to the dice world. He is an out standing player in his own right.

Soft Touch, Michael Vernon and **Pablo** often assist **Dice Coach** and are three renowned shooters. **Stanford Wong** of blackjack fame is an accomplished craps shooter along with **DaveofSA.** When it comes to practice DaveofSA is one of the most dedicated players I know or have had the pleasure of playing with.

TinHornGambler is one of the finest gentlemen you will ever meet at a crap table and is a long standing member of the dice community. He can shoot too!

My partner in the Dice Institute web site, **DeadCat,** is also an all-star shooter close to being a full time crap player. You have to be good to spend as much time as he does playing craps.

The **Mad Professor** is one of the most well known all-star craps player that nobody knows. His writings preceded him and bring to the dice community a vast amount of craps knowledge. His entire manuscripts can be found at Diceinstitute.com. He is the feature writer on the web site.

The Saturday night boat crew is slowly making its mark on the dice community in the Midwest. The original crew consists of **Target, Laser910** and **Charlie009.** All three have had fifty roll hands along with one of my students **Fiftyroller** who had a fifty-six roll hand at the Westin three years ago. The other crew members in training are **Longshot, Swick** and rookie **Radar.**

Clubsodakenny, a crew member in waiting, deserves big thanks for proof reading this book. Thanks **CSK!** Your dedication to the game shows in the fantastic craps table you maintain in your home. **CSK's** generosity in making his table available to the Midwest Boat Crew has improved their shooting immensely.

Seas3to5 better known as **Super Rick** is a Vegas local who is an expert on flea control along with his shooting ability.

There are other all-stars in the dice community but I haven't played with them enough to judge their craps ability. Those mentioned with the exception of one or two, I have played with and feel they deserve all-star status for their contributions to the dice community. If I missed someone it was probably intentional or I was having a senior moment.

I have often been asked who the best players are that I have played with or witnessed their craps ability. There is no way you can rate one player better than another in this game. Of all the players mentioned in this book, I would not rate one better than another because of the nature of the game.

Each individual is good in his own right and has contributed to the dice community in his or her own way.

No one knows who the **Mad Professor** is, but his writings speak for themselves. His unselfish sharing of his detailed knowledge of the game is beholding to all of us. What makes the **Mad Professor** unique to the game is that nobody knows who he is. He is known for his knowledge of the game and not for whom he is or what he has done.

When is comes to teaching craps one on one, there is no one more adept at it than the **Dice Coach**. I have had the pleasure of attending and assisting him in some of his seminars. **Dice Coach** is recognized as one of the premier instructors in Las Vegas area.

I have had the pleasure of playing and learning from other instructors in their own right. **Irishsetter, MadDog, Heavy, Soft Touch, and Michael Vernon** each teach their own style of playing craps.

I would be glad to share a table with any of the twenty-five people mentioned in this chapter. They all can run the table at any time and proved they not only talk the talk but can walk the walk.

Note:

Several of the "All Stars" are experts in various phases of becoming dice influencers and advantage players. I have asked a few of them to write a chapter on their field of expertise. I felt that impute from some guest writers would provide craps knowledge other than my humble opinions. In some of the following chapters you will hear from the dice community's best at what they do. (009)

Chapter 48

Boat Report, a Lesson Learned

May 8, 2009

I had only been to the boat once since Spring Fling and was anxious to go when Jswick called to see if I was interested in joining him and Longshot. They also wanted to know if they could warm up on my table before we left.

I agreed and we spent a half hour tuning up our tosses. We arrived at the tables at noon and found only three of the ten tables in play. They had one $5 and two $10 tables loaded with randies .We noticed they were getting a forth table ready to go so we inquired how long before they open up. We were told ten minutes.

Longshot spotted a female suit he knew and went over and exchange hugs. Longshot introduced us to the suit and she asked if we needed any thing. I suggested they reserve out positions while we wash our hands.

When Jswick and I returned, there was a chair on each side of the stick with a towel on the chip rack at our spots.

We settled in and started buying in. I inquired who the first shooter would be. The stick person pointed to Longshot and said he was the first to buy in so he goes first. Longshot says, let Jim shoot first (SR2). The crew went along with this.

We learned something new already. When a new table is opening up, the first person to throw the dice is the first person to buy in. Longshot remembered how long we had to wait for the dice to come around in the past. The table was filling up and at lest we will now have the first three turns with the dice.

The first go around was make a few numbers, the point and seven-out. The second round was my best with the dice. I had the Iron Cross set up and held the dice 25 minutes. The third round Jswick got hot and went on a six and eight binge and made a point four for good measure. The forth round Longshot took over and threw a lot of numbers which had Jswick and me on the field bet. The fifth round was a bummer. We all went point seven-out.

Looking back at our loss we made the same old mistake we always make. We bet on too many random rollers. We got too comfortable at that table with the super table crew we had. We had the opportunity to get away with a small win but we stayed and gave it back. We did however have dinner on the house.

A point learned! When starting out at a table about to open, make sure you are the first to buy in. That way you get the dice first...

Chapter 49

Another U-Boat Adventure

June 5, 2009

Longshot calls at 3 p.m. and says he is five minutes away and do I want to go to the Boat. I said, "Are you crazy, five minutes away? Of course I will be ready.

We landed on the shores of Lake Michigan around 3:45 p.m. and still marveled at the big building with attached garage that they call a boat. It wasn't crowded at all. Longshot jump right in his position at SL-1. I went to the powder room to wash my hands so as not to dirty the dice. When I came back there was a towel on my position at SR-2.

I just got settled in when Longshot decided to go table hopping. He had the misfortune of throwing one too many sevens at the wrong time. He went to a table that was just opening. I stayed where I was with the dice only two players away. I had a respectable twenty minute run including three points and a bunch of six and eights

I looked over where Longshot was and he was waiving for me to come over there where I found another one of those white towels in my spot. LS had just finished a good run and asked the pit critter to save my spot. This has become a good ploy of ours especially when they are about to open a new table. With the suits so friendly we might as well push the envelope as far as we can.

The table was filling up fast along with some familiar faces that seem to follow us from table to table. At my end of the table they were coming and going and some were playing with short stacks and passing the dice.

At the other end of the table a couple moved in with a short stack of red ships. The female, wife, girlfriend or whatever got the dice and proceeded to throw some numbers. After her seven-out the guy took some chips out of her rack for the pass line. The stick moved the dice to him and I asked if it was fair for the two of them to play out of the same rack with everybody waiting to shoot the dice. He said it wasn't his call. I dropped the subject not wanting to draw attention to myself.

Back to the U-Boat! A lady at my end of the table shooting from the dealers hook was spraying the dice all over, mostly off the table. Once she threw the cubes high and wide and one bounced off the rail in front of the guy at SL-3. He took a swing at the die and missed by at least six inches. The die landed back on the table and the box guy called, "Good roll, seven-out. " The guy that swung at it went ballistic. H insisted that the die hit his hand. The shooter kept yelling no roll. Somebody else yelled keep your dam hands to yourself. While the box was arguing with the jerk, the stick and I agreed he missed the die by at least six inches and what difference does it make anyhow? The cube landed on the table and was in play.

You know who won that argument! When the jerk got the dice the box was all over him to hit the back wall and keep the dice on the table. It takes a lot to get these box people mad, but when they do, look out.

Things settled down and we got back to some serious up and down craps. We were approaching the three hour mark and getting tired and hungry when the female suit came around the table and tapped me on the shoulder. She said, "Charlie, surveillance just called down and said you look hungry and to give you a dinner comp. It could only happen at the U-Boat. Now that I think of it, was it a ploy to smooth things over at the table? It got everybody laughing.

When we left the table and were exchanging farewells, I gave the thumbs up salute to the ceiling cameras. Another laugh and we were gone.

Chapter 50

Dave's Practice Ability to the Top

DaveofSA is one of the dice communities most dedicated students of the game of craps. Practice is his middle name and winning is his game. His hours of practice and his thirst for dice knowledge have made him an all star in the dice world. His desire to learn and give something back to other craps players is recognized and appreciated. I have had the pleasure playing and socializing with Dave over the years and would belly up to the table with him anytime. (009)

I received a Private Message (PM) today from a really good friend of mine, Charlie Westcott. Yes, that's right, the author of this book. He asked if I'd be interested in adding a chapter in his latest book – his fourth on Craps. It took me about 2 seconds to respond in the positive. First off anyone who's met Charlie knows it's just about impossible to say "no" to him. He is one of the nicest guys you'll ever meet, whether it's at a craps table or just in life in general.

But what am I to write about? As I sit here in front of my computer I did not know where to start. I am well known for my practice habits so I will concentrate on that part of the game.

My beginning in craps is a little muddy as to when and where it began.

I had only played craps twice before I found out about the world of Dice Influencing (DI). So I really believe my life as a Craps Player began on February 26, 2006. This is when I stumbled across this internet board about DI'ing and Advantage Play for Craps. This is where I learned just about everything I know about the game of Craps or at least this is where I got pointed in the right direction. This board is run by "Heavy" a DI coach and general Craps expert.

I started reading and asking a thousand questions. Finally one of the Board Members, Wild Child, suggested that if I were serious about becoming a DI, I needed to go to Tyler, TX. This is where Heavy lives' and sometimes he can be coaxed into giving lessons in his own home. I contacted Heavy and the trip was on.

I had scheduled 2 hours with Heavy but before I knew it, it was close to 4 hours. Just a few of the things I learned that day: Good eye-to-hand coordination is a must – golfers, bowlers, pool and dart players all have a good chance at becoming a decent DI. BUT and it's a BIG BUT – very few have the time and discipline for what it takes to become proficient at Dice Influencing. Over the next few months I would spend countless hours in my dining room (this is where I set up my practice rig) tossing the dice.

Here is how it plays out: you need to simulate tossing in a casino at a craps table; you toss the dice from a tossing station to a receiving station, approximately 8 feet away. If the dice happen to stay in the receiving station you don't have to bend over to pick them up. If they do not, you get to chase them down, bend over, pick them up and do it all over again. You must also record the results. As you become proficient in the tossing of the dice (we are talking months of 2 to 3 hours per day – 7 days a week) the analysis of the toss results become as important to you as the toss itself.

The worst part is – we DI's are never satisfied. We will change our stance. We will change the way we grip the dice. We will change the trajectory of the flight of the dice. We will change the position we shoot (toss the dice) from. Any change just about negates most of the toss data that we have collected – so we get to start again.

For every hour I have spent tossing the dice I have spent 30 minutes analyzing the data. Why? This data should give me a good idea of the results I should be able to achieve in a casino, shouldn't it? The answer is yes and no. Not all tables are the same – some are too hard, some are too bouncy; some are too short, some are too long; I think you get the picture. Dice influencing is not a perfect art form.

One thing we do practice at – both dice must hit the back wall. There is a misconception out there by many casinos that we (DI's) intentionally attempt to "short roll". A short roll is where one or both dice fail to travel all the way to the back wall. I do not know where it is written that both dice must hit the back wall – but if this is what the casinos want, this is what they should get. After all it is their table.

After seeing Heavy toss I really got the feel for what a good toss should look like and I was off and stumbling. If there was a mistake to make I made it. I wouldn't settle on a toss, grip, stance or location to toss from. But I had seen it ("it" being a proper toss) done and I knew I had above average eye-to-hand coordination.

During my time in the military, the United States Air Force sent me TDY (temporary duty) several times just to throw darts. I would win the base level contests and then travel to represent the base I was stationed at. I played on many in leagues in the U.S. as well as in Europe. So I knew the eye-to-hand coordination was there.

As my practice became routine I started to show some positive results. The Great American Crapshoot (GAC) was coming up and I had planned to attend but like any red blooded American I was worried about how I would fair meeting 30 or so people that were obsessed with the game of craps like I was. So I made an appointment with "The Dice Coach" in Las Vegas. So I flew to LV to spend some time with TDC. TDC – Beau picked me up and drove me for a 2 hour lesson in his home.

Beau asks me what I wanted to get out of this lesson and I told him that I didn't want to embarrass myself at the GAC. We started the lesson off with Beau just watching me toss. He decided that he liked me tossing from Stick Right (SR) better than from Stick Left (SL).

At this stage of my DI'ing I only tossed using the Over Hand (OH) grip. Now with the OH grip you can use a three, two or one finger front (the thumb is always in the back with this grip). I had progressed from the three to the two and finally the one finger front. As I type this, today, I only use the one finger grip when using the OH grip.

The two hours with TDC are still with me to this day. He "tightened up" my grip and corrected the trajectory of the flight of the dice among many other adjustments. At one point he had just a piece of paper about the size of a pencil eraser at the end of the table and told me to "hit it". I was thinking that it would be next to impossible to hit it with any consistency. I actually managed to hit it a few times. Today I can wear out any target for 8 to 9 feet from me; I have holes in my table to prove it. TDC told me that he didn't think I would embarrass myself at the GAC.

During this trip to Las Vegas, where I spent time with TDC, a friend (non-craps player) and I were getting our butts kicked in Let It Ride. I noticed a craps table with only one player at it. I told my friend that I know how to get our money back. I took him to the craps table and he decided just to watch. I will not go into all of the details but when I finished my one and only hand I had not only gotten my money back, from the Let It Ride butt kicking, but I had enough to purchase myself a full size craps table – and I did. I had a blast with this hand, when I finished the table was jam packed with players. During this stage of learning about being a DI I wasn't very smart about betting and to be honest I was betting very stupidly and would never do that again today.

A few months later it was time for the GAC and my first ever meeting with Charlie, he'd told me where and when for TSOMM and myself to meet up on the first day of this trip. Charlie and his bride showed up right on time and almost the first thing out of his mouth was "have you two eaten yet?" We had not and he says "Let's go" and he heads for the Steak House and we run into two more friends of his on the way so we now have a party of six. As we are seated Charlie gets a phone and calls his host and tells him he wants this dinner of six comp'd and he gets it.

Charlie and I shoot many times together over the next three days. But the funniest is when we didn't. We meet up Saturday morning and as luck would have it the Craps tables are empty so I "belly up" and Charlie announces that he needs a cup of coffee and heads off to Starbuck. I don't drink coffee so I take the dice. When Charlie returns about 20+ minutes later I am coloring up and he asks if I am leaving to which I tell him that I have had only one hand during the time he was gone and that I had doubled my buy-in and it's time for my breakfast. Charlie looks at his coffee cup and declares that it's the most expensive cup he's ever bought – he'd missed my money making hand.

Charlie is a great guy to play with. I don't recall ever seeing him upset at anything, he's very even mannered. I am high-strung and I have a tendency to let "things" get to me. But I will not shoot when I am tired or hungry. I avoid tables that are crowded with non-DI's.

It was at this event (the GAC) where I started taking the recording of my in-casino tosses very seriously. In all of my Trip Reports (TR's) I only report on tosses (hands) that are witnessed. If other DI's didn't see the toss – it didn't happen. It was also at this event where I became known in the DI community.

In our first scheduled gathering – the night of the day I arrived, I was really just a guy who posted a lot and asked all sorts of questions. As a table opened everyone scrambled for positions – the better shooters normally get first choice. I was moved around more than once to get these known shooters in position. I finally got the dice from SR-2.5 and had one of the better hands of the night. I was tired so I didn't stay long, but the next morning when we all got together for the official start of the GAC I finally got to meet and put faces to the many BM's that I had been in communications with.

The GAC (seminar) is scheduled for 2 days, and there are 2 events that are scheduled for fun and a few bucks can be made. One of the events is the No 7's Contest. We see who can toss the longest without the 7 being tossed. I finished 3rd and this was to set the theme for the next two seminars as I was to always finish

3rd (only the top two make any money). Also the first one to toss a 7 gets his entry fee back. I have stopped entering this No 7's Contest. The second and biggest of these events is the Golden Arm's Championship.

The Golden Arm Championship: This contest takes place in a casino, at a craps table, with everyone's money on the line. The shooters are assigned their positions by Heavy and his coaches. The contest is really very simple: You have all of your new friends at a table with you, their money on the line at risk just like yours and if you are one of the assigned shooters you are expected have a decent hand. If you do not, you will be replaced from one of the shooting positions. I keep the award as Golden Arm Champion in my study with my table. As side note: Someone had a better hand than I did, but Heavy wanted to present the award not receive it.

For those who wish to learn a bit about becoming a DI the two best places I know of are Charlie's Board: http://diceinstitute. proboards.com/ and Heavy's Board:

http://axispower.proboards.com/. At Charlie's he is assisted by The Mad Professor and Dead Cat. Dead Cat has the unfortunate roll of handling the day to day activities on this board. Heavy has a good handle on his board and the duo Irishsetter and Maddog are there when he isn't and they are at the top of the food chain when we are discussing anything about the world of the DI. It would take several weeks of concentrated effort to cover all of the material on these two boards. On top of that if you are not familiar with the terminology you could get totally confused.

There is one thing you should really understand about DI's, very few are able to make money playing craps. We as a group are action junkies. While we may have a small edge on a number or two, the majority of us give up this edge, and more, while betting on non-DI's. And if this isn't enough very few DI's take the time to study and learn just what their edge is.

Since my journey began I have gone from the rookie of all rookies to someone who has tried to give back as much as I have received. I make my mobile number known to many BM's as I see them begin their journey. I consider myself lucky to receive countless emails and PM's. I answer them all. Not just because I feel obligated as a long time member of the boards I mentioned above but because so many took the time and effort to help me as I began. I just figure it's time for a little pay back.

Now for a little bit about practice. Practice is really where all of the work gets done. Live casino play is the reward for all of the practice.

What I will cover now is just a bit about practice. Anyone with any intentions of learning the art of Dice Influencing you have got to get your head wrapped around the idea of countless hours of practice.

First you must be ready to practice, by this I mean mentally and physically. You need your practice to mimic your casino play as much as possible. I have two types of shoes that I wear whenever I have my money at risk. I wear loose fitting pants and shirts. I don't want anything to be tugging on me. I don't play when I am tired or hungry, why should I practice in these conditions? I don't.

In live play there are all sorts of distractions and here I have plenty as well. From the wife, son and 4 dogs –I think every practice should be with a purpose. The purpose will change as a DI's skill level progresses. At first just getting the dice to stay on the practice rig seems to be a big accomplishment. During my trip to Tyler I'd seen Heavy toss using a practice rig and I knew it was possible but it sure was frustrating when I'd toss the dice and I would end up having to chase down the dice, for once they bounced off the practice rig and on to the floor there was simply no telling where they would end up. I ended up putting a few towels on the floor around my rig to stop the dice from bouncing all over the place.

One of the basic concepts that are hard to translate into action is energy. The Mad Professor has written an entire series of articles about Conquering Ultra Bouncy tables and in this series is the underlying message is the "Low Slow and Easy" (LS&E) toss. I had been practicing for months and was getting some very interesting results. Then I had the chance to see Irishsetter toss – I just thought I knew what LS&E was.

I'd had lessons with Heavy and The Dice Coach. Their methods were to take it easy on this rookie and keep it simple. I had private time with Irishsetter and Maddog. I had private lessons with the four best teachers in the business and I was doing extremely well at the tables. However, I was just standing at a practice table and Irishsetter walks up and starts tossing the dice. Just those couple of minutes of me keeping my mouth shut and just watching him "warm-up" changed how I would toss - forever. Energy, rotation and trajectory (ERT) would now be important parts of my practice. These three have to work in harmony to achieve the toss that we are looking for. I have constant access to Heavy, The Mad Professor, Irishsetter and Maddog. These are the four main sources I turn to when I have a problem. Also I have been helped by hundreds of members from Heavy Axis Power Craps board and Charlie's Dice Institute craps board. Their names are simply too numerous to mention and more than one or two of them would wish to remain anonymous.

Notice that I said ERT would be a part of my practice – what I mean is that it would be part of my unconscious practice. When I am at a table with my money on the line I don't know want to be worried about these items, they should be as natural to me as breathing is to everyone. Proper breathing is something I will touch upon a little later. Today I am a "feel" shooter; I have spent thousands of hours at my practice table. Today when I am asked about my grip I have to look and examine my own grip. My grip just "feels" so natural I don't think about it I just do it.

For a DI the grip is where 90% of all problems begins and end. I'll get a call "Dave my left die is off axis twice as much as my grip die, how I fix this?" Most DI's problems are with their grip. A simple sliding one finger about 1/32, one way of the other, will work wonders.

Energy is one of these things where less is better. We want to get the dice to the back wall with the least amount of energy possible. Energy is also one of the things that can get us in trouble with the casino if we don't use it correctly. The correct amount of energy must work in harmony with the rotation and trajectory.

Rotation; Most shooters use an Over Hand Grip/Toss. This toss induces backspin on the dice. During this toss the dice rotate backwards. This backwards rotation – backspin – can help stop the dice. Most DI's use 2.5 to 3 rotations of the dice, I use 3 quarters to 1 full rotation. (Note: the amount of rotation should and does depend on the shooting position of the DI and the table conditions.)

Trajectory will vary from DI to DI by a wide margin. I think many DI's overlook the importance of their trajectory. For the most part when I am tossing, the dice will just barely get higher than the rail of the table

Practice is where the grip, energy, rotation and trajectory of the toss come together. As I mentioned earlier the beginner's practice can be frustrating. I'd seen these great shooters doing things that by watching my practice you'd have thought (I know I did) was next to impossible. During my practice I was "inventing" new four letter words. For the remainder of this chapter I will be practicing on a full size 12 foot regulation craps table.

All good practice starts with an in balance stance. I am right handed and the most comfortable shooting position for me is from Stick Left (SL), I stand next to the Stick Man, on his left side. (Note: for this article I will be tossing Over Handed only.) When I talk about someone joining me at a table I tell them to "belly up". What I mean by this is that most Craps Players actually have their bellies leaning up against the table at some point at the table. For a DI I mean this literally. I stand with my toes in line and pointed toward the dealer opposite me and I am leaning into the table. This eliminates any movement from my lower body. Think of it like this – the fewer parts I have moving the fewer things I have to keep in coordination with each other.

Not much to the stance is there? Well I wish things were this simple all the time. Most DI's should and do only shoot from one position. I do things the hard way and I toss from just about anywhere and this causes some problems. When shooting for Stick Right (SR) my foot work is entirely different. My right foot is pointed toward the dealer opposite of me and my left foot is pointed toward the Stick Man next to me. This opens up my stance and allows free and easy movement of my tossing motion. Side note: My lower back is metal and it's pretty stiff and this stance, from SR, allows me to turn easily without putting any pressure on my lower back. We don't really need to "practice" the stance. We simply want a stance that is stable and consistent.

Gripping the dice; When the Stick Man moves the dice to you, as the shooter, gripping the dice in a quick easy motion is very important. Many of the complaints about DI's (often we are call dice setters) are mostly about the amount of time we spend setting the dice. I carry a set of dice with me everywhere I go and when I have a few free minutes I take them out and I "set" them. I will not be going into the 6 primary dice sets and the hundreds of permutations that are available to the DI. A good DI has studied his practice results enough to know which ones should be working best for him. With two moves of any one die should produce the results the DI wants to see. This setting of the dice shouldn't take more than 3 seconds. I practice this all of the time.

A beginner DI will be worried to death about the results of his toss. For the beginner this should be the last thing to be concerned with. I would suggest that after the beginner has gotten his stance down and can set the dice with efficiency he should start to concentrate on just how is he picking up the dice – the grip. The over hand grip has the thumb in the back and one, two or three fingers in the front. The DI will have to decide which is best for him. Keeping the finger balanced and aligned is a constant and ongoing battle for all DI's. Deciding where the fingers make contact with the dice is another choice for the DI. These decisions normally are decided on what feels comfortable to the DI.

Again I practice my grip as I practice setting the dice, it doesn't have to be done at the practice table.

Now we get to a two items that are hard for the beginner to overcome. First is the thumb, as you start your forward motion and it comes time to release the dice, your thumb will want to "push" its way through and between the two dice. The results will be the dice separating as they fly through the air; this is not a good thing. I can live with minor separation of about a quarter of an inch, anything more and we have a problem. A beginner will have to consciously think about not moving his thumb. After many hours of practice this, not moving the thumb will become natural. The second item to worry about is the wrist. A DI will want to flick his wrist at the time of release – it's a natural motion. This flicking of the wrist adds unwanted and unneeded energy to the toss. I actually wore a wrist band for several hours to help me eliminate this flicking of the wrist. The thumb and wrist are necessary evils. They are required and needed for the toss but too much participation by either or both is a serious problem. You can get all of the energy you need for a good toss in a slight raising of your arm, mainly for the elbow on down there should be a slight movement, also for the shoulder joint.

The coordination of the above from the stance to the releasing of the dice can produce a good looking toss of the dice. But all of the above doesn't do the DI any good if he can't hit the Landing Zone (LZ). The LZ is an area the DI needs to have the dice make contact with the table. As a DI progresses the LZ is shrunken down to what we call the Landing Spot (LS). The LS is about the size of a silver dollar. A practiced DI will hit his LS 80+% of the time.

At times I will just pick up the dice and toss just to hit my LS. If I can toss the dice and get three quarters of a rotation and they get no higher than the table rail, hit my LS, the dice should bounce one more time just prior to making contact with the back wall. The dice should have enough energy remaining to bounce off the back wall and come back 3 to 6 inches. A couple of years ago I wanted the dice to die at the back wall, but today the casinos are wanting the dice to rebound a bit further. The thing is – you want the dice to have the same amount of energy and act and react together. We DI's, have a primary goal of "a repeatable toss." If a DI has a repeatable toss – shouldn't the results be repeating as well?

If you stand at the same spot, the same way; set the dice the same way, grip the dice the same way, toss and release the dice the same way; hit the same spot on the table, what do you think will happen?

If you go out and buy a practice rig and start to practice – don't expect miracles over night. I practiced 2 to 3 hours a day everyday for months. I had the help and support from many great Dice Influencers.

A typical practice session:

I am well rested, fed and ready. I will make sure my LS is well marked. A set of dice will last from 500 to 1,000 tosses. The casinos give me dice that are in good shape and their edges are sharp to toss with at their tables. My practice dice are also in good shape. There are distractions in casinos so I leave the door open to my study. The sounds, disruptions and phone calls that happen during practice are all part of practice. I have pen and paper available to track each and every toss I make. My rule is if I set the dice then I record the toss.

Before I begin practice I must decide why I am practicing. What toss do I want to practice, the Over Hand toss, the Under Hand toss or the Axis Grip (Pincer) toss? Where do I want to practice from, SL1, SL2, SL3, SR1, SR2, SR3 or from SO? SL3 would be to the left of the Stick Man 3rd position down, SO is straight out at the end of the table. 99.99% of all DI's should only use one type of toss and toss from maybe two positions, this is one of those cases of do as I say not as I do.

Normal practice is from Stick Left 2 (SL2) Over Hand. I use my middle finger and thumb only; this is often referred as the OH one finger toss. A typical session is 72 tosses. If I have missed a day or two, of practice, these 72 tosses will be to hit my LS. Usually this only takes me a toss or two to start to nail down the LS. Once this is accomplished I concern myself with the flight of the dice and this includes their rotation and the trajectory. This again should not take me more than one or two tosses. As the dice hit and make contact with the table I concern myself with just how they are making contact. By this I mean are they landing "flat" or on the edges – exactly what part of the dice is making contact with the table first. After they make contact; just how are they proceeding to the back wall and where are they making contact with the back wall. After I have completed the 72 tosses the real work begins – the analysis of these tosses. However, I am not really super concerned with just 72 tosses. 72 tosses are too small a sample for me to come up with any data that might change my betting plans. And let's face it we practice to learn what and how to bet.

For the beginner it might take 4 or 5 sets of 720 tosses to have any meaningful data to work on. But really the true beginner should not be worried about their toss result he should be worried about achieving muscle memory for a repeatable toss. If a shooter can achieve a repeatable toss, he is then on the border on becoming a DI (Dice Influence).

The hardest thing for a DI is not actually tossing the dice, but recognizing what his dice are doing and making adjustments in his betting to pull a few bucks of profit off a craps table. Back to this, 99.99% of DI will stand at a craps table and give his winnings back to the casino by betting on those who are not DI's.

Are you too lazy to practice? Not a problem. When you are at a craps table and you see some dude setting the dice and they are hitting the same spot regularly; check out how he is betting, you just might want to be the same way he is.

The Craps table can be a scary thing for the first time player. I know. It was for me. Let me invite you just walk up to a nearly empty table (totally empty would be best) and ask a dealer how the game is played. The dealers stand next to the Box man (he's the guy sitting down). The dealers are there to help you and watch all bets on their side of the table. The Stickman (the person with the stick) is busy following the dice and keeping the dice moving. To join a table you simply watch the dice and the dealer, when the dice have been moved near the Box man. This is when you lay your buy-in down in the "come" area along with your player's card and say "change only, please." This tells the dealer that you only want chips and are not making a bet at this time. Tell the dealer that you don't know anything about the game but you'd like to "place the 6 and 8 for 12 each" and place a green chip down in the "come" area and you are playing craps. Just a quick side note all of the bets in front of the Stickman and Boxman have high casino advantage, stay away from them. The Stickman will ask if you want to make a "C" and "E" or" other such nonsense, just smile and shake your head "no.

I will leave with this story on a DI not hitting the back wall. This shooter, we'll call him XXX, practices and plays mainly on 12 foot tables. Well here we were in Las Vegas at a 14 foot table and he "can't" reach the back wall. His muscle just will not allow him to toss the dice that far. By the time he has received his 5th warning he has made his 6th point. The rookie Boxlady announces "Okay that's it we are passing the dice." How would you like to have to finish a hand like that? The table is jam packed, thousands of dollars are at risk, XXX has made 6 points and all of a sudden you are the shooter! Join me at the tables sometime and I will let you know how I did.

DaveofSA

Chapter 51

The Darkside of Craps

There is an old saying that if you want a good job done surround yourself with experts in their field of expertise. When it comes to playing the Darkside of craps there is none better in the Midwest than "The Golfer". I have asked him to enlighten us on how and why he plays the Don't! (009)

Don't Pass (DP) and Don't Come (DC) bets in the game of craps are two great bets in the casino that most people do not make and never intend to. Playing Don't bets is commonly called playing the Darkside. Hello Darth Vader.

Depending on who you talk to, Darkside players are, crazy, evil, stupid, antisocial, traitors or scum. Most players feel Darksiders are cheering them to lose and accuse them of making a table go cold, losing money for all the other players. I have seen players walk away from a table cursing if a Don't player starts to bet.

The reality is a far cry from the perception and Don't players are really human. They are just trying to do what everyone else in the casino is trying to do, get some of the casino's money.

I began to take a look at the darkside shortly after riverboat gambling became legal in Illinois in the early 90's. Up until that time my gambling was limited to infrequent trips to Vegas and

231

vacations where there was legalized gambling and my method of play was always "with" the dice, on the Rightside. Yeah, I did play craps and 21 on my honeymoon. Doesn't everyone?

With the chance to play more frequently I also found the opportunity to lose more frequently. In these early days I found that in many cases, shooters who tossed the dice with a repeatable soft motion seemed to have longer rolls and made more money. I tried to do the same but I was still losing more than winning

At this time I did begin to notice a person or two playing the Don't. My 1st reaction was who the hell were they? Yet, as I saw more I realized they had chips and I didn't. I also had learned at this point that tables went choppy or cold and just betting with the dice was a really bad idea at times. I liked to play. I hated to lose. I forced myself to give the dreaded Darkside a chance to see what happen.

My first DP bet was a table minimum. I was scared to death but the dice favored me and I won the bet. I was playing in the top of the hook, next to an older guy also playing the DP and he coached me some and took some of the nervousness away. Another thing that helped me was that I kept winning. I don't remember the amount I won that day but I felt like I had just discovered the secret of craps.

As the years went by I trained myself to play the Darkside and shoot the dice in a controlled fashion. This shooting technique was called "precision shooting" in the early days and now goes by the handle, Dice Influencing (DI). Today I play mostly the Darkside, when I bet on others and when I have the dice I will bet the Rightside and the Darkside, depending on my mood, the conditions an the session bankroll that I have in front of me. What follows is a recap of what I have learned so far with Playing the Darkside of craps, and a few suggestions for those who might want to leap into the abyss.

How To Play The Darkside

Playing the Don't is easier than it looks. Almost all of the darkside bets you can make are "Self Service" bets (like field bets) that require you to place your chips within a certain area, namely the DP line and the DC box. There is another bet called the "Lay", which is placed against a certain number. For these bets the dealers must set them up behind the box. We will mention these later.

The basics are real easy. You lose your DP/DC bet if a 7 or 11 is rolled. There are three (3) craps numbers but the casino only lets you win on two (2) of them. They bar the 2 or 12, meaning if that number is thrown the Rightside bettors lose their come-out Pass Line or Come bets but the Darksiders get a tie for no blood.

If any number besides a 2, 3, 7, 11 or 12 is tossed on the Come-out, that number becomes the point. The Darksider wins if the 7 rolls before that particular number. This is really good stuff. Why? Every time you get a point set for your DP or DC bet youve the advantage. You now have more ways to win than lose.

This is based on the combinations of two six sided dice, which provide 36 possible facial combinations.

The beauty of the above is that your DP/DC bet is paid off at even money. Now this isn't true for odds bets on the Don't, but it is true for the base or "flat" DP/DC bet.

To Lay Odds or Not To Lay Odds

Like Rightsiders, Darksider bettors are allowed to wager additional money on their flat bet by the Casino. The big difference for Darksiders is that on DP/DC bets you have to lay **more** than you will win. Using the chart above, if your DP bet is for a point of 9 and you wish to add a lay odds you must lay your money at a ratio of 3-2. For every three chips you bet you will be paid two chips on a win. These are true odds and there is no advantage to either the casino or the player, according to the math.

Even though there is no mathematical edges to lay odds they are a bet that offers one feature that the corresponding DP/DC bets do not, namely there is no come-out to survive.

You put your odds lay out there and they only way it will lose is if the shooter makes that point. Unlike a flat DP/DC bet, the 7 will actually win this bet for you and remember what we said above? You always have an advantage when up on a point.

The controversy on this issue is that DP/DC odds **always** are paid at true odds, meaning you have to bet more than you win. For this reason many Darksiders will not lay odds. In my own mind, lay odds are worth it for two reasons:

1. Your bet always has a mathematical advantage.
2. You get more money into play when you have an advantage.

One of the greatest Darksiders of all time was Nick the Greek. According to urban legend, he supposedly said near the time of his death that if he had it to do over again "he would not lay odds". Some take that as gospel and play the same. Others lay odds and take what they can. This is a personal choice based on your own gambling personality and bankroll. *(Authors Note: Nick the Greek died broke.)*

Come-out Danger

In talking up the beauty of the Darkside, I do not want to create an impression that it is a no lose strategy and it is the shortcut to massive riches. There are dangers and the biggest one is the shooter's come-out roll.

Reviewing, the 7 and 11 are death to the DP/DC bets. The 2 and 3 are winners (when the 12 is barred).

The DP/DC are great bets, but that only holds if they survive their come-out roll.

Hedge the Danger

Darksiders, like their Rightside brethren, like to hedge against losing on the come-out.

Hedging can work well but it comes at a cost. You can hedge but it will reduce your overall profitability.

I do hedge playing the Don't, if the table tells me to. During a particular session I will easily see and feel a trend on come-outs that feature 7's or 11's. I will be losing. In these cases I will hedge if the trend is still favoring the Don'ts after the come-out. Many times you will observe a trend that produces come-out winners for the Rightsiders but no point made. That is golden to a Darksider, if he can find a way to get thru the come-out.

My hedging strategy usually focuses on preventing damage from either the 7 or the 11.

If 11's are showing on the come-outs and taking my DP down I will size a prop bet on the YO (eleven) to cover my flat DP. A $15 (or less) flat DP gets a $1 YO bet. If I go higher on the flat I will make a $5 horn hi yo bet and also try to capture some extra cash from a hit on a 2, 3 or 12.

If the come-out killer is the 7 I will put out a **Lay Bet** on the come-out, betting a properly sized Lay against a single box number to protect my flat DP.

The Art of A Lay Bet

Not mentioned above is another method of hedging against the 7 and that is a bet on the Big Red (Any 7) or a Hop bet on the 7's.

I do not use this method as it is a one roll prop bet that always loses or wins. My preferred method is the Lay Bet. The selling point to me is that if the 7 is not rolled on the come-out I do not lose my hedge. Every math guru will tell you that hedging dilute profits. Ok, who am I to argue. I will use a hedge method that offers the chance to **not** dilute profits (if it doesn't lose).

Is this some new discovery that will revolutionize the game? Not at all! Is it a guaranteed money saver technique? Not at all! What it provides is a hedge for your come-out DP/DC that you might not have to pay for if a point is set. Here's how it works.

8A Lay bet can be made at any time and is set up by the dealer in the DC section of each box number (behind). The casino will allow a Lay bet but you have to pay the vig on it like a Rightsider pays the vig on a "Buy" bet. The cost ratio on a lay bet vig is how much you will win, the exact opposite of the ratio for the Rightside, which is based on how much you bet.

Lay bets, like buy bets are paid at true odds. On Lay bets you always bet more than you win. You will win lower amounts on the

4 and 10 than you will on the 6 or 8 because there are more ways to lose the 6 or 8 than there are the 4 or 10.

So when I start to use the Lay as a hedge I will make my flat DP bet and then size a Lay bet on the 6 or 8 to cover the DP. If I have a $25 DP I will use a $30 Lay on the 6 or 8.

I will put the chips in the field or come areas and tell the dealer "$30 no 6". I will actually put down $31 because I know that I have to pay the vig upfront.

If a 7 rolls I lose my DP but the dealer will cut out $25 and ask if I want to stay up. I will say yes and then replace the $25 DP bet just lost with the winnings from the Lay. I will have to pay another $1 as vig.

I use the 6 and 8 as the lowest cost options The math supports the 4 and 10 as the better bets, yet if you lose a 4 or 10 it hurts more financially.

If during the session I start to lose my Lay bets, but want to continue playing, I will move my Lays to the 5 or 9 to see what happens. A perfect method? No, but is mostly works for me. If you try this method and your Lay keeps getting hit and you are losing it almost all the time, you really need to consider if this is the table you want to be playing the Darkside on. It might be time to end the session or transition to the Rightside.

Hedge the Hedge

Some players are so risk averse that they will hedge their hedge. In this case what they would do is make a bet on the DP or DC, set up a Lay bet on a number like the 6 or 8 and then they would hop the 6 or 8 with a properly sized bet on the hardway/easy ways to save the cost of the Lay bet if the 6 or 8 show. I will admit that I have done this on rare occasions. I did not hop all the ways on my Lay number but rather would make a hop bet on the hardway of the 4, 6, 8 or 10 to protect the Lay if the hardway hit. It is a cheap bet at a great payout but the HA is so high that it is a long term big loser. I would only use this in those rare sessions where it seemed that every point was set with a hardway being rolled. Like they say on TV, "don't' try this at home".

Find A Darkside Method That You Can Live With

Like the Rightside there are an assortment of betting styles and strategies out there. Any one will work at some time. What you have to do is find one that makes sense to you and run with it. At the present time I am using what has been labeled Dave's System, named after a local Illinois player who had success with it. I have had the chance to play with Dave and see it work. The system is no special secret, but is basically a 3 Point Molly on the Don't.

You make a flat bet on the shooter's come-out roll. If you win with a craps you same bet the next roll. If you lose to a 7 or 11 you replace the bet. If you get a point set you place as much of an odds lay as you like and put out a DC bet for the next roll. Rinse and repeat on every single roll thereafter Dave doesn't stop at 3. He also has a couple of his own variations. If two (2) of his bets with odds lose he takes all remaining lay odds down, leaving just the flat DP/DC bets up. He then stops and waits for the 7.

In addition to this, Dave will not lay odds on 4's or 10's. It is just the way he plays. He has been successful with this play and has done well. Will it work for you? Maybe! Maybe not.

The Final Darkside Word

I have played craps for over thirty years and have won and lost. That's the way the game goes for most. I do believe there are three things that players can do to improve their chances for profits.

1. Learn how to influence the dice (DI).
2. Learn to play the Darkside.
3. Learn real money management.

Dice Influencing can work.

I have made it work. I have seen it work. Few can achieve the highest levels and only do so with a tremendous effort, practice and dedication. Face it; there are not a lot of Michael Jordan's or Tiger Woods walking around. You can achieve some level of capability with effort and once there you need to maximize your skill level with proper betting and discipline.

Learning to play the Darkside makes a player two dimensional. Instead of just losing money or walking away when a darkside wind blows, those who have developed darkside skill can position themselves to recover or profit for a session or sessions. Like DI it takes effort to learn and discipline to practice. The best method is combining DI shooting with darkside betting.

Making money management a priority requires a new way of thinking. Discipline is never easy but if you examine anyone who has ever been called a winner in any endeavor you will find discipline in abundance. Manage your money and you will be there for those great rolls or trends and you will put yourself into position to profit.

Craps is a negative expectation game. DI, Darkside Skill and Money Management can give you an edge with an effort. Good Luck!

Golfer

Chapter 52

Determining Your Edge
is Crucial,
But Distracting Yourself from
Winning is Ridiculous

The Mad Professor is one of craps most knowledgeable members in the dice community. I felt that this book would fall short of its expectations without a chapter from his vast archives of craps knowledge. "009"

The Mad Professor Speaks-- -- --

As dice-influencers, it is *crucial* that we determine how big of an edge we have over the house, and to bet our advantage in a compelling way.

Similarly, it is important that we determine how *frequently* any of our proposed bets are expected to hit during the life-cycle of a typical hand, and how much net-profit it will generate when considered over a reasonable number of in-casino trials.

However, there is always the temptation to over-analyze our skill-set to the point where it ends up distracting us from actually winning anything.

The old-school guys call that ***analysis paralysis***.

Ascertaining and verifying how big our edge is and how frequently it will manifest itself, is a *good thing*.

Being paralyzed by over-analysis and getting caught up in trivial minutiae to the point of distraction is a *bad thing*.

Dice-influencing comes down to **THE TOSS**.

Once you have the ability to de-randomize the dice, then it becomes a matter of properly exploiting those de-randomized results through matched-to-skill wagers.

Although it is important to consider all the factors that are either *contributing to* or *detracting from* our dice-influencing performance; there is a fine line between studied *reflection* and *over-* over-analyze way too many extraneous factors and not look closely enough at how your toss is actually working; it's easy to lose sight of the objective as we make busy work studying and scrutinizing the smallest-but-unusable detail in our toss-stats.

As an advantage-player, I want to know where my strongest edge bets are, and I want to know how frequently I can expect them to hit .Sometimes we get so wrapped up in breaking down and analyzing everything, that we lose sight of the most important factor that will get us to our objective.

Develop a ***good, solid, repeatable consistent toss***, and then make the ***bets that are best suited*** to that consistency. It's not rocket-science, so there's no need to calculate whether that edge will hold up in a parallel universe where each dice has nine faces or on Alpha Centauri if they ever open a casino there in a zero-gravity environment.

Back here on earth, you simply need know where your strongest edge bets are, and how frequently you can expect them to now that football season will soon be upon us again, I'm reminded of the questionable handicapping/trend-spotting skills that accompany a lot of the football-pool and television color-commentary:

"Well this quarterback tends to throw much better when the opponents team has at least three or more vowels but less than three syllables in it's home-town name; however that's only applicable if they're coming off of a road victory where they beat the other guys by more than 15 points, and where the half-time show included a

marching-band, two jugglers and a clown...otherwise, his pass-completion rating actually goes down, unless of course the Dow Jones Industrial Average has seen a 1.7% move in either direction over the last 72 hours, which will trigger his running skills which haven't been tapped since his junior year of high school, in which case....this game will be A LOCK!"

If you need to know to *a certainty* that your D-I skills-edge will hold up to within one-thousandths-of-one-percent over 8-billion throws; then the casino is *the last place* you should be.

Just as football is a game of blood, snot, and tears; dice-influenced craps is a game of skill-deviation, edge-variance, and transitory profit-opportunities.

You have to be aware of your skills and the advantage over the house that those skills offer; but you can't get bogged down in the investigative, overly-analytical stage forever...you eventually have to actually *exploit* that edge in the casino.

Paper-analysis has to be balanced not only with dice-in-your-hand *practice* and refinement; but it also has to be interspersed with real in-casino trials where you *re-validate* and *re-verify* all the ciphering' and figuring that you've been doing at home.

The more genuine practice that you put in on your at-home rig, and the more *real-world verification* of those skills you gain in the casino; the less time you'll need to figure out what the hell went wrong with your toss and where the hell your money went.

I'll be the first one to tell you that you have to determine *what* your edge over the house is in order to turn your skill into profit; and I'll readily admit that I am also a huge proponent of looking at that advantage in fine enough detail so you can properly *exploit* it on a consistently profitable basis

However, I can also say in all sincerity that while determining your edge is *CRUCIAL*; Distracting yourself from winning is *RIDICULOUS*.

Good Luck and Good Skill at the Tables...and in Life.

The Mad Professor

Chapter 53

The Evolution of Your Skills

Looking through the Mad Professor's archives I discovered another gem that speaks for it self. Words of wisdom that should be followed by everyone. ((009)

The Evolution of Your D-I Skills Often Require Evolution of Betting-Methods...as well as Evolution of Your A-P Beliefs.

Think back to where your dice-influencing skills were one year ago.

Have they improved at all? Has your understanding of how dice-influencing works, and how best to optimize your skills when you have money on the line, changed at all in the last year?

If you've been at this for longer than a year; has your appreciation for the finer points of *nuanced advantage-play* changed at all since you began this journey?

If there is one thing I have learned about the whole art and science of de-randomizing the dice, it is this:

Evolving D-I skills often require evolving BETTING-Methods, as well as *evolving, updating, and refreshing* your advantage-play IDEAS and BELIEFS.

Evolution is part of the whole dice-influencing experience, and as your shooting-skills improve; it is absolutely *necessary* that your betting-methods and your understanding of how best to optimize bankroll growth, *evolves with it.*

Five years ago, I looked back on the five years *before that* and I figured my shooting had advanced about as far as it was ever going to get...and I was quite happy with that.

Now, I look back on how far my shooting has advanced even further over the last five years, and I can't believe how much it has improved...and again I am quite happy with where it is now.

Will it continue to advance and evolve? Almost certainly!

The same holds true for my betting. That too has evolved so much over the last ten years that it bears absolutely no resemblance to how I was betting 10 years ago.

The same holds true (but not as dramatically) for the last 5 years. For example, back then, I never would have thought that my **Table-Adaptive Field-Harvest** method would be able to produce an average of +3.8 net-hits per hand ('net-hits' are the number of Field-wins minus non-Field losses including the final hand-ending 7-out).

Another example would be how tightly-focused my betting has become. Six years ago, I never would have believed that I could make more money by *staying* on my top two or three box-numbers (and using a portion of the profit from *prior sessions* to up their *starting-values*, instead of being overly concerned with pressing them up with just-won same-hand profits) and instead of spreading out to more and more numbers.

It took me a while to wrap my brain around that, because the 'non-exorcised gambler' in me found it to be somewhat counter-intuitive, or at least counter-gambling-instinct

In fact, I think *that* in itself may be one of the chief reasons why many skilled D-I's are so reluctant to change the way they bet too. They see an outcome that they don't have money on, and they feel like they're 'missing out', so they put money on that one. Then the next outcome reveals another number that they 'need' action on. A couple of rolls later they go with a hunch and put some money on another new one too. Soon they have *all* bases covered, so that nearly any outcome will produce a payoff; yet they can't understand why they never seem to make enough money...or at least as much money as their talented shooting deserves.

Advantage-play dice-influencing *DEMANDS* that our betting methods evolve as our skills improve and our knowledge-base advances.

Another example of how *evolving skill* and *evolving understanding* of optimized advantage-play has affected my game, is in the number of *hours* that I play per week, as well as how constantly evolving skill and a clearer understanding of optimal advantage-play has affected my *hourly earn-rate*.

I guess we could break it into two parts; *Pre-WONG* and *Post-WONG.*

A couple years before Stanford Wong's *Pi Yee Press* published my book, we would have long back and forth discussions about all things *"Dice-Influenced Advantage-Play."* This went on for months and months.

Let me just mention a couple of things that came out of all that *challenge-the-status-quo* and *justify-where-your-money-is-invested* discussion:

WOTCO.(Working On the Come-Out) Now the *concept* of WOTCO isn't new, nor was it new back then; but the idea of *abandoning* the idea of treating the Come-Out cycle and the Point-Cycle as separate *"Game Within a Game"* elements, and treating them both as part of the same *bet-when-and-where-you-have-the-BIGGEST-overall-advantage* was new to the dice-influencing community. In other words, using the C-O as a *PRE-extension* of the actual point-cycle, actually adds a much steadier (and net-larger) stream of profit to your bankroll than the occasional bigger-but-rarer GWAG-win does.

~Field-Harvest. This was one of those serendipitous finds that often come out of free-flowing discussions (I intentionally left out the word 'intellectual' from that phrase for fear of offending anyone who objects to free thought). Stanford was talking about some experiments he had been doing with the S-6 (Straight-Sixes) dice-set, and they just happened to coincide with some that I had been doing too (but on an entirely different D-I thesis). When we looked at the Foundation Frequencies and at the resulting edge-per-roll

that that S-6 set generated; we both reached the same, *"MP should be harvesting the Field-bet,"* conclusion.

Now as far as hours-of-play per week is concerned; I came to find that if I concentrated most of my 7-exposure money on my top two or three highest-advantage numbers (instead of spreading the same money too thinly across too many box-numbers, as I had been doing); I could generate *far more money* **much faster.**

I'll candidly admit that I was *extremely* reluctant at first about cutting back on my bet-spread. I mean, I was making *great* money off of my *widely-spread* box-number action, and frankly I didn't see the full benefit of the trade-off (though academically I understood what *SW* was continually driving at); so I gave it a try.

The rest as they say is history.

Once I validated that approach for myself, it was just a simple matter of putting more money where it would do the most good, and reducing it (or completely eliminating it) from where it wouldn't.

Now I know that *sounds* simple, but you have to remember that I was doing pretty freakin' good *without* Wong's advice, so it was a huge leap of faith for me to even *try* some of his advantage-betting ideas out.

As a scale of comparison; *Pre-WONG*, I had been playing 30 to 35 hours per week...*Post-WONG*, I was able to ratchet it back to 25-to-30/week...then to 20-to-25...then to 18-to-20/week...and now to my current level of around 15 hours per week., all without reducing my net D-I earnings at all.

In fact, by ratcheting *up* (and super-focusing) my **bet-values,** while simultaneously ratcheting *back* my hours of play; my hourly earn-rate has actually increased exponentially.

What's the upshot of all of this?

Evolving D-I skills often require evolving betting-methods as well as evolving, updating, and refreshing your advantage-play ideas and beliefs

Good Luck and Good Skill at the Tables...and in Life.

The Mad Professor

Chapter 54

Searching for the "Holy Grail"

The search for the "Holy Grail" of craps won't end in this book. The only way you will have a chance on catching lightning in a bottle is to stand in the rain under a tree till it sinks in that only practice will give you a small edge to make a short term gain at the table.

There are hundred's of systems out there touted by other writers and web sites. These systems are all doomed to fail. If these systems were any good everybody would be using them and the casinos would be closing their tables.

The methods of play discussed in this book are examples of how you can incorporate them into your play based on your signature numbers developed with hours of practice.

PRACTICE is the only short cut to giving yourself a chance to turn the odds in your favor. No other short cuts or systems will work.

The object of this book is to give its readers a chance to learn good practice techniques and other craps information that will help their game. With proper practice techniques the reader has a chance to become an advantage player that the casinos will fear.

To be good at any sport you have to practice. The players that practice the hardest are the one's that win the most championships. The readers that practice the most are the ones that have winning sessions more often than others.

My tip of the day is to practice and keep practicing until you can make that beautiful toss with your eyes closed and then practice some more.

Chapter 55

The Dice Institute
Website and
Members Forum by *DeadCat*

DeadCat is one of the premiere craps players living in the Las Vegas area and currently playing full time. I asked him to write a chapter about the "Dice Institute" and how it can be used as another tool to educate the new player on advantage play..(009)

When Charlie first suggested that we start a website and message-board I thought he was joking. After all, there are already several and the best at that time, Dicesetter had done a great job of providing free information and great member-supplied content, but had fallen apart in a matter of months after its creator "IrishSetter" had sold it to an instructor with a very different outlook. I had been a moderator on that board and its demise had been tough to take.

But, after I thought about it I told Charlie I'd do it, with one condition; that we bring on The Mad Professor and make the site his home. Charlie agreed and we set about getting the "M.P.'s" participation. That was September of 2006. We launched the message board in November and with some technical help our free content web site, the **DiceInstitute.com** went live in February 2007.

With contributions by Charlie, the Mad Professor and others, the DiceInstitute.com quickly became the largest *FREE* source of information on the newest "Advantage Play" (AP) method, many call "Dice Influencing" or DI for short. I know Charlie is proud of that, as am I. We feel that anyone who can make money at a craps table as an AP shouldn't need to "sell" information to raise money. The Message Board at URL: **http://diceinstitute** .proboards.com/index.cgi is accessible by subscription only, which funds the main, free web site and charging a small ($24/year) fee keeps out the spammers and flamers. We also agreed to be generous with our "comp" policy which applies to about half our members. In essence, if you join and become a contributor of quality posts, we waive dues as long as you continue contributing good posts.

All in all it has worked out pretty well. We are able to provide new articles on the free site all the time, thanks to both Charlie and M.P. being prolific writers. On the message board the members are constantly both helping and pushing each other to continuously improve and refine our skills, all with the goal of changing a game of luck into a game of skill and making it pay.

Currently we have over 350 members adding more on a weekly basis. In the 2+ years we've had the web site and board up and running we've seen advancements in world of "AP Craps." Members are always experimenting with new shots and betting techniques and the more "senior" members and moderators, like Charlie and M.P. are always there to help the "newbie's.

I think that's what I'm proudest to be part of, a small community that works to improve itself and does so in a mutually supportive and open-minded way. And one that does what they say can't be done.

We don't give seminars or sell betting "systems." The money we take in is just to keep the free site open and each year we take what's left over and host a (free) party in Las Vegas for our members. This year we were able to keep a hospitality suite open for the 50-60 members and friends who came though. Most took the opportunity to compare sets, grips and tosses and to hit the tables as teams, both large and small.

I live in Las Vegas and play full time. I've met a large number of our membership. More often than not, I am impressed with the serious, level-headed approach our people take to craps as an AP opportunity. I honestly believe that most of them can be successful with practice and discipline and am always happy to hear stories of their progress and keep an open ear for innovations they make.

Looking forward, I fully expect our site and board to remain on the cutting edge of this exciting opportunity, where good shooters can legitimately develop skills that make a card-counter's edge look small. And if it never grows past the 350+ members we now have, that's OK too. Either way, Charlie, M.P. and I will be there to make it the *best* resource for those seeking to turn this game of chance into a game of skill.

I hope to see you at the tables. *DeadCat*

Chapter 56

The Bum Dice Question

Once in awhile I get questions about loaded or shaved dice. All I can say is it's possible but I have never witnessed or come in contact with any in casino play. A year or so back I purchased a stick of red dice and a stick of gold dice. Longshot was over for a practice session and said he thought the gold dice were smaller.

Sure enough you could feel the difference. The red dice were .75 inch and the gold dice were smaller. The gold dice although smaller could still meet special specifications. There doesn't seem to be any universal accounting for size between customers and Manufactures.

For practice purposes just make sure you have two die that have the same manufacture number. It's easy enough to check the number on the casino dice in play when you are the shooter.

While in Vegas I talked with some friendly dealers about the dice. The consciences were if any casino messed with the dice they could lose there license. The percentages are stack so much in favor of the casino they don't have to cheat.

You might find in under financed grind houses some questionable games, but that would be rare.

Six days in Vegas and I didn't see, feel, or smell any bum dice. But then I forgot to bring my micrometer and balance caliper. The first thing I did when I got into town was buy two sticks of red dice off Dice Coach. I was going to be prepared incase I run into some of these shaved cubes that is on some people's minds. Foiled again! Where I did most of my playing at Monte Carlo, they had blue dice. Oh well, the next time I go there, I'll put some blue finger nail polish on my new dice just in case I don't like their dice.

On one session at MC, I was busy throwing numbers all over the place and making points like you wouldn't believe. A suit came over and sat down at the box, relieving the box person. Fiftyroller pointed that out to me and said be careful. During a lull in the action, I said to the suit, did I do anything wrong? He said no, he just didn't want to miss any of the action.

I can't say I was in the zone because I was hitting chips in the mine field and hiding the dice behind the dealer's chips. I was really enjoying myself. I had the Iron Cross in full bloom and the numbers kept coming.

Then it happened! I launch the most beautiful on-axis spiral the world has ever seen. The cubes went rotating side by side in perfect unison and made a three point landing perfectly in the target area and eased into the bottom of the back wall and came to rest 3 inches out from the wall, side by side.

I couldn't believe my eyes when I saw 2, 5 looking straight up at the ceiling. The dice were even embarrassed. It was a toss you dream about. I felt like throwing up on the table. If I could have gotten my hands on those dice I would have tossed as far as I could. Maybe it was shaved dice.

Chapter 57

Clubsodakenny has worked his way to the forefront when it comes to experience on building craps tables. His current 12 ft table rivals anything you will play on in Las Vegas. In order to become the best practice facility you can afford, I asked CSK to enlighten us on what it takes. (009)

Building a Table and Practice Rig

Charlie009 asked me to put together some thoughts on how to build a crap table and practice rig so I harkened back to building my first crap table and how I got interested in Dice Control. To give you a little background I became interested in Dice Control or Dice Influencing during the summer of 2005. I had read a number of books about craps and decided it was time to take a class and to start building a casino crap table. Now I am lucky enough to have plenty of room in my basement and I didn't have to ask permission from a wife. So I ordered a set of plans on the internet for about $49.00.

Knowing that I may embark on building a table I decided that I needed to know more about craps tables so I did some table recon in the casinos and surfing the net. After reviewing the plans that

I ordered on the internet I also decided that I needed to expand the table from its six or eight feet length to a more casino like ten foot table complete with chip racks and drink rails. I also decided that I needed to make the table heavy duty just like ones found in a casino.

I also figured at some point I would have the fellas over for a craps night and with that thought in my mind I figured that I needed to build the table rock solid. In my minds eye I pictured twelve of my buddies leaning on this table so having it build rock solid was very important to me. After making the necessary structural changes as well as the dimension changes I started to compile a laundry list of lumber that was needed to build the table. The plans that I ordered on the internet contained some paper templates. These paper templates were to be traced onto the wood and then the wood could be cut to size and later assembled. In order to incorporate the changes I had to make some modifications in the paper templates.

In preparation of writing this chapter for Charlie009 I went back and checked the receipt from that first trip to the Home Depot. Here is that original list of lumber supplies.

10 - Sheets of ¾ inch 4x8 Sheets of Oak Plywood
16 - 8 foot sections of 2x8's
6 - 1 ¾ inch Flush Hardwood slab doors

As with most "do it yourself" projects I also spent a great bit of time traveling back and forth to the Home Depot. When it was all said and done it cost me almost $2000.00. Now I am not gonna lie to you but this project gave me plenty of excuses to go out to the Home Depot and buy some new power tools.

I set out to make a really sturdy base for this table and had made a few recon trips to local casinos in order to observe the different styles of legs and various leg supports and cross beams. It was fun trying to get a good look under the crap tables not in use in the casino without alarming any casino pit bosses.

After that I set out tracing all the templates onto my plywood and making the necessary cuts. I decided that I needed to shape the table legs similar to the H-style used by some casino manufactures.

I shaped the legs and bolted on the mounted supports using joist hangers and 2x8's. I also bought some "L" brackets to secure the bed of the table to the base/legs.

Now I have to tell you I went a little over board on building the craps table bed using 1 ¾ inch Flush hardwood slabs that are commonly used as doors. I mounted the hardwood slabs to the "L" brackets and then it was time for getting the table level and make sure she was all square. The table bed template already allowed for the drink rail to be part of the craps table bed. I think it is really important to get the bed of the crap table at the height of about 28 inches as most craps table in the casinos are around that height.

After the bed of the table was done it was time to build the side rails, back wall, and dealer positions. The hardest part was making the curves in the hook position. I was lucky enough to have a friend who used his band saw to help pre-shape some of the pieces which cut down on the time I spent finishing and sanding. After securing the side rails and back walls we had the crown almost complete. I needed to build some chip rails which means clubsodakenny gets to buy a router with some really cool bits. After routing out the chip rails it was time to mount the chip rails to the crown of the table. I then sealed and finished the wood portions of the table in a flat polyurethane sealer. I also used some silicone based adhesive to secure the rubber pyramids to the back walls and hook positions.

With the crown ready to be mounted I needed some help stapling the felt layout onto the bed of the table. Prior to laying the felt down on the bed of the table I laid out some sheets of newspaper (three to four sheets) as an underlayment to the felt. When it came to stapling the felt down it took three sets of hands to get the felt stapled nice and tight and most importantly straight. Once the felt was stapled down, I figured that as long as I had the extra sets of hands available it was time to mount the crown to the table.

When the crown was finally mounted on the table we enjoyed a few good tosses of the dice however I knew that we were not finished. I still had to add the arm rest pad on the top by the chip rail and I also wanted to put the same padding along the drink rail. I went to a local fabric store and bought some foam padding and heavy duty Naugahyde type vinyl covering. It took some doing and a steep learning curve to staple the padding and vinyl where it looked good and was functional. Again when it came to stapling the vinyl padding a second set of hands sure made it easier.

Once the table was done it was time to get back on the internet and order some more dice, chips, pucks, and a stick. The boys and I had a heck of a party to break-in the new craps table.

After practicing for almost two years on my home made table I decided that in order to further improve my toss, I needed to upgrade my practice equipment a little. I felt like if I wanted to take the next step in improving my toss it was time to buy a regular casino 12 foot table.

After a lot of thought I felt if I really want to get better and consistent I needed to buy a 12 foot casino crap table. It was a very difficult decision for me as I had put a lot of blood and sweat into the 10 foot table that I built. I shopped for about two months on-line checking various websites prices and delivery date availability. Some of the guys from The Dice Institute message board (thanks to Dave of SA) and a few others guided me through the purchase of a 12 foot table.

Once I began to practice on the 12 footer casino table I began to see subtle improvements in my toss. As time has gone bye I have continued along the dice control journey. Recently my toss is more consistent these days and in fact I have been working on becoming more toss proficient on 14 foot tables. If you can conquer the 14 footers also, it opens up more quality shooting opportunities in the casino...

Now I realize that most people just do not have the room for a regular casino 12 or 14 foot table. Reason being once you move a casino table into a regular sized room it fills up the room pretty darn quick. I was lucky that I had enough room for a 12 foot table. You never really realize how big a casino crap table is till you try to put it in a room in your house.

I also know quite a few guys who are tossing everyday on a practice rig and they have great consistent tosses. While I never owned a practice rig I have practiced on them and I think most handy guys should be able to build one by streamlining the full size table building project.

I think most guys could build a practice rig by using ¾ inch plywood mounted on a folding table legs or building a table top version. Some guys use the ¾ inch plywood doubled up back to back so the bed of the rig is more casino like in its bounce characteristics. I also want to advise the "do it yourselfers" to take into account the thickness of the bed so the rig remains 28 inches in height.

You can go to your local fabric store and get some good quality felt to cover the base. I would recommend keeping your practice rig as close to your local casino playing conditions in regards to the bounce characteristics. You can use three or four sheets of newspaper as an underlayment underneath your felt.

I also have seen some DI practice rigs set up on pool tables as well as mounted onto a pool table base. Again, if you can you want to keep the bed of the table at around 28 inches above the floor.

For the DI's who do not enjoy the thrill of building and setups. There are also some very talented folks out there something with your own hands there a number of websites out on the web that sell practice rigs and shooting stations in varies sizes building and selling half craps tables with shooting stations on the internet.

Clubsodakenny

Author's Note -

For those of you who lack the necessary skills to make your own craps table, you might try buying a second hand table. One of our esteem colleagues, DeadCat, did just that. He pulled off the caper of the year when he purchased his craps table from a casino. What makes this so outstanding is how the purchase played out.

The casino maintenance guys brought the table over to DeadCat's abode in three pieces and assembled then in DC's second bed room. The casino included a second, still unwrapped, custom made felt top that he plans on having the casino guy install.

With a little initiative you can sometimes accomplish what at first seems unlikely. "009"

Chapter 58

The Final Word

Can we control the dice? The answer is no! There is no way we can have absolute control over the end result of a tossed pair of dice. That being said, we can however take steps to attempt to influence the out come by the way we set and throw the dice. We can set the dice so fewer sevens will be expected.

By keeping our tosses on axis by developing muscle memory and developing a consistent throw, we enhance our prospect of a favorable result. The toss is the key to consistent results.

You can't go out there and say, "I'm going to throw a seven." You have one expected chance in six of doing so. You would be better off saying, "I'm going to throw a six or an eight." You have one expected chance in four of doing so.

My point is to get you thinking about what set is best for obtaining an expected result. Our main object is to throw less sevens than the next guy. The casinos say it can't be done. Then why do they get so paranoid when some one gets on a hot roll?

They tell us to hit the back wall with both dice. Don't they know that's exactly what we are trying to do? We should thank them for the advice. Remember, craps ability is derived from sense ability to give your game credibility.

Good luck and good shooting.

Afterword

After all has been said and done and you have memorized this book you will at least have the knowledge to proceed towards becoming an accomplished Advantage Player. You are going to have to resign yourself to many hours of practice to develop a consistent toss. The toss is the backbone of the Dice Setter skills. All the other knowledge you acquire will be of no avail without that envied toss. Practice it till you can hit your target zone blindfolded and then practice some more. Some say it can't be done. Prove that the naysayers are wrong.

Glossary

Terms and Handles Used in this Book and Outside:

ACTION—The bets you make or the fights you get into with players.

ANY CRAPS—A one roll bet looking for a 2, 3, or 12 and the guff you take from the pit critters.

ANY SEVEN—A one roll bet looking for a seven that is hopping.

BAR 12 -- Disadvantage to the Don't Pass and Don't Come better. A 12 neither win nor lose.

BETTING LIMIT—Maximum bet excepted on any number. -- Amount of money in your pocket.

BOX PERSON—The lazy guy seated at the center of the table, who watches everything that transpires in a craps game.

BUY-IN—The amount of chips you acquire when arriving at the table.

BUY THE FOUR OR TEN—Paying a 5% commission to the casino in order to be paid the correct odds of 2 to 1 on placing the four or ten.

C&E or CRAPS-ELEVEN—A bet that 2, 3, 11 or 12 shows on the next roll of the dice.

CHARLIE009 -- PHD—Doctoral of Dice Influencing.

CHICKEN FEEDER—A random roller who throws the dice like he or she was feeding chickens.

CHIPS—Tokens issued by the casino in place of money, having the equivalent of cash

COLOR-UP—Having your chips of small denomination changed to chips of larger denomination so you won't have so any to carry to the cashier's cage.

COME BET—After the come out roll, it is a bet that the dice will repeat a number.

COME BOX—Area on the table layout where a come bet is made.

COME-OUT ROLL—First roll of the dice before a number is established.

COMPS—Receiving complimentary meals, rooms, points or service which are given to players for their action.

CRAPS—When a 2, 3, 12 shows on board and the player swears.

DEADCAT—My partner on Dice Institute.com and a formidable shooter in the dice community.

DEALER—Person who handles all your bets and pays you when you win. He will answer all your silly questions.

DI—Dice Influencer—One who tries to change the outcome of probability.

DICE—A pair of cubes with numbers indicated by dots called pips, which are rolled to determine payoffs and loses. The numbers on each side of the dice always total seven.

DICE COACH—Premier instructor and one of the top shooters in the Las Vegas area.

DICE SETTER—A shooter who meticulously sets the dice a certain way before each roll.

DON'T COME BET—A bet made after the come-out roll, that the shooter will not make his point.

DON'T PASS BET—A bet made on the come-out roll, that the shooter will not make his point. The bet can be taken down at any time.

EASYWAY—The opposite of hard-way. Rolling a 4, 6, 8, or 10 without throwing a seven.

EVEN MONEY—Being paid at 1 to 1.

FIELD BETS—A bet that the next roll of the dice will come up 2, 3, 4, 9, 10, 11 or 12.

FIRE BET—Betting that you can make four, five, or six different point numbers before you seven-out.

FIVE COUNT—After a point is established, a count of five rolls is waited on, before placing anymore bets.

FLOOR PERSON—The person that approves your credit, rates you on your play.

HARD-WAYS—A wager that dice will come up 2-2, 3-3, 4-4, or 5-5 before the seven comes up or the number is made by other combinations.

HIGH ROLLER—A better that bets large sums of money. He is sometimes known as a whale.

HIT—A number rolled, that pays off.

HOPPING SEVENS—A bet that the seven will come on the next Roll in a certain way, like 4-3.

HORN BET—A one roll wager on the 2, 3, 11 and 12.

HOT ROLL—Dice that are continually passing and held by the same shooter for a long period of time before the seven out.

INSIDE NUMBERS—Numbers 5, 6, 8 and 9.

LASER910 -- Midwest player and member of the "crew" with tons of potential.

MAD PROFESSOR—Could be the best dice mind in North America.

LAYOUT—Imprint on a felt surface covering the craps table.

ODDS—The correct ratio determining whether or not an event will occur.

OFF—A call by a player that his bet will not be working on the next roll of the dice.

ON—Bets working.

ON-AXIS TOSS—Toss that rotates with backspin on both dice and remain together till landing side by side.

OUTSIDE NUMBERS—The numbers 4, 5, 9 and 10.

PASS—A winning decision where a shooter makes a point.

PASS LINE—The area on the table layout where a pass line wager is made.

PAY-OFF—To be paid on a winning wager.

PIT BOSS—Supervises all craps tables in an area called the pit. He handles anything that the floor manager can't.

PIT CREATURES—They are the guys in dark suits, standing behind the craps tables drinking coffee.

PLACE NUNBERS—PLACE BETS—A wager on the numbers 4, 5, 6, 8, 9, and 10 made in the place box on the layout.

PLAYER—Gambler or better who puts money where his mouth is.

PLAYER CARD—Plastic card that looks like a credit card, that is turned in to the floor manager at the table games for tracking your play for comps.

POINT—The number 4, 5, 6, 8, 9 or 10, when rolled on the come-out.

PRESS—To increase a bet by one unit or doubling the bet.

PROPOSITION BETS—All bets in the middle of the table.

RACK OR RAIL—Grooved area at the Craps table where you place chips not being bet.

RHYTHM ROLLER—A shooter who rolls the same way time after time.

RIGHT BETTER—One who bets with the dice.

RR—Random Roller is a person who throws the dice any old way.

ROLL—A single roll of the dice or a series of throws, until the shooter sevens-out.

SEVEN-OUT—Throwing a seven after a point has been established, ending the roll.

SHOOTER—Player who throws the dice.

SR—Stick right—The first shooting position to the right of the stick person facing the box person.

SL—Stick left—First shooting position to the left of the stick person facing the box person.

SUITS—The pit critters with dark suits and bored looks on their faces.

STICK PERSON—Calls the game and uses the stick to move the dice to the shooter.

TABLE MINIMUM—The least amount of money you can bet at the table.

THE CREW—Chicago area original players still playing; The Target, Laser910 and Charlie009.

THE CREW IN TRAINING—Clubsodakenny, Longshot, Jswick,

Fiftyroller and Radar.

THE TARGET—Out of the GTC school and plays craps eight days a week.

TIP OR TOKE—A gratuity or bribe given to a dealer to leave us alone when we are shooting.

U-BOAT -- Harrahs Horseshoe Casino, Hammond Ind.

UNIT—The basic amount wager on the pass line, come or place area.

WORKING—Bets that are in place and can win or lose on the next roll of the dice.

WOTCO--Working On The Come Out.

WRONG BETTER—One who bets against the dice.

Half Table Layout

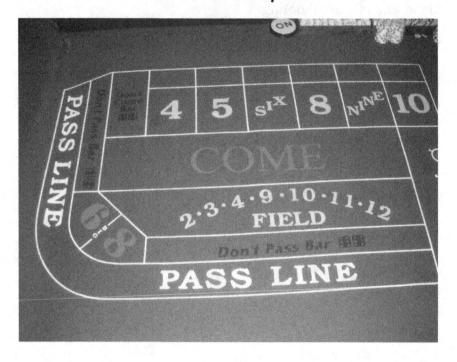

Join
The Dice Institute

The largest free source of Dice Influencing / Control / Skilled / Precision Shooting Anywhere!

JOIN NOW! www.diceinstitute.com

Other Books by Author

Book 1 -- "Crap Shooters Wake Up and Smell the Roses"

ISBN 1-58808-104-6
Book 2 -- "Craps and Smelling the Roses"

ISBN 1-50129-478-9
Book 3 -- "Wake UP Crap Shooters" Books by Author
- ISBN 059390083

Available at: Amazonand Barnes and Noble.
- iUniverse